# THE COMEDY OF EROS

# THE COMEDY
# OF EROS

## Medieval
## French Guides
## to the Art
## of Love

TRANSLATED BY

*Norman R. Shapiro*

NOTES AND COMMENTARY BY

*James B. Wadsworth*

UNIVERSITY OF ILLINOIS PRESS

*Urbana, Chicago, London*

# Translator's Preface

A NY TRANSLATOR WILL APPRECIATE THE ADVAN-
tages of working on a medieval text. There
are no nasty copyright problems, no out-
raged authors to decry the mutilation of their off-
spring, not even any descendants to voice the au-
thors' outrage vicariously.

On the other hand, there are certain endemic dis-
advantages. No translator, as a matter of principle,
can please everybody. But for the medieval transla-
tor it is especially impossible. Some readers insist
that any medieval text be approached with rever-
ence and awe, and demand an unadorned, almost
literal translation. Others prefer an "artistic" rework-
ing that would nearly relegate the original to insig-
nificance. Some are of puristic bent and would pre-
fer a translation with a clearly archaic ring, hewing
as closely as possible to the form and language of
the original. Others feel that only a jazzy, modern-
idiom version is acceptable to today's readership.

I think I have maintained a middle ground. Al-
though the originals are not presented here for com-
parison, it should be apparent that I have not at-
tempted a word-for-word translation. On the
technical side, I have preserved the rhyme and
metric structures of the poetic originals, at least
insofar as syllabic French verse can be brought over
into English. As for the language, it is certainly not
archaic, but neither is it excessively colloquial. I
would like these translations to be readable twenty-
five or fifty years from now, as well as today.

To be sure, I have had to take a number of liber-
ties in following this middle ground. Like most

medieval texts, these are not without their problematic passages, due either to the many nuances of the ancient language that may escape us today, or to simple scribal carelessness. I have used my best judgment to interpret and fill out such passages, rather than remaining stubbornly "faithful to the original" by leaving them to their ambiguity. Occasionally, too, even the poet seems to have a lapse. Maître Élie, for example, is not above omitting the second line of his couplets now and again, and the anonymous author of *De courtoisie* goes him one better by adding a third to his when the mood hits him. In such instances I have also violated the sanctity of the original by restoring the couplets in question to their time-honored length. As for a more general liberty, I have leaned a little to the side of assuming some of these texts more humorous perhaps than their authors intended. The reader is warned. Not all the verses should be taken as gospel. Still, while I may have played a little with some of their spirit, I think I have remained quite faithful to their letter.

These translations were prepared with the aid of a Ford Foundation grant, awarded through the National Translation Center, for which assistance I am especially grateful. I must also thank Professor James Wadsworth—present at the conception, gestation, and birth of this volume—not only for providing his excellent scholarly introductions and notes, but also for dissuading me, with his impeccable good judgment, from appending to it the subtitle *Octosyllabic Coupling in the Middle Ages* (along with other possibilities that I have since put from my mind). My thanks go also to Professors Caldwell Titcomb and Evelyn Simha, and to the many other friends, academic and otherwise, who have patiently and unflinchingly let me subject them to my frequent readings, and whose reactions to them were always of great value. I am particularly grateful as well to Dallas Hext for her expert typing of the manuscript for publication.

As ever, I wish to thank my parents, whose encouragement has been the major ingredient in this, as in all my work.

Norman R. Shapiro

Middletown, Connecticut
September 1970

# Introduction

THE MIDDLE AGES IN FRANCE—THE AGE OF FAITH
—were fascinated by love. Love in all its man-
ifestations, from the crudest expressions of
physical realities to the loftiest heights of mystical
union with the Creator, penetrates the hearts and
minds of the era. In southern France the trouba-
dours, according to one influential critic,[1] invented
romantic love, that force which ennobles man as it
makes him subject to the will of his lady. In north-
ern France there were born romances that still de-
light readers with tales of Tristan and Isolde or of
Lancelot and Guinevere. Lyric poetry, lengthy ro-
mances, and shorter tales speak everywhere of love.
Scholars have striven to find the origins of this
courtly love—the term is a nineteenth-century in-
vention [2]—and to define the characteristics that set
it apart from purely animal cravings. Its sources
have been sought in classical literature, in medieval
Latin literature, in the poetry of the Arabs, in the
social conditions of southern France, even in the in-
fluence of the Crusades; in short, everywhere imag-
inable, and without clear triumph for any school
of thought. In defining the concepts of courtly love,
scholars have met with little more success: courtly
love has always existed as far afield in time and
place as ancient Egypt and tenth-century Iceland,
says a recent critic; the term is artificial and a posi-
tive obstacle to our understanding of medieval texts,
says another.[3]

Whatever solution wins our personal preference,
these disputes testify to the enduring fascination of
a rich and vital literature. We still tend to see it

through glasses tinted by English Romantic poetry, by Pre-Raphaelite art, and by opera. There is, however, another side to this medieval preoccupation with love: a desire to teach it as an art, to present a set of precepts and rules for its proper exercise. In this, as in so many other aspects of medieval French literature, *Naso magister erat*, i.e., Ovidius Naso was the teacher. It is significant that Guillaume de Saint-Thierry, abbot of Rheims (d. 1148), cannot even bring himself to mention the name of Ovid, as he testifies to the success of the Roman poet, "doctor of the art of love," in teaching the "filth of foul carnal love": a success so great that Ovid himself had to offer his own Remedy.[4] Despite monastic repulsion, Ovid's works were, in fact, so seriously studied and imitated, in both Latin and the vernacular, that a great medievalist, Ludwig Traube, has called the twelfth and thirteenth centuries the *aetas ovidiana*, the age of Ovid.[5] For the Latin master offered poets whole stories to imitate—*Pyramus and Thisbe, Narcissus*—and he showed them in detail how to depict the joys and anguish of love. He also bequeathed to them his *Ars amatoria*, intended, for Ovid's sophisticated contemporaries, as satire and as a comedy of manners, rather than as a serious handbook for the young lover. In two books Ovid tells how to find and win a mistress, and how to keep her affections. As an afterthought, he adds a third, to teach the girls how to catch and keep a man. The *Ars* proved as irresistible as his other works. The greatest author of romances, Chrétien de Troyes (fl. late twelfth century), made a translation of it, now lost. In the following century, Maître Élie, Jacques d'Amiens, Guiart, and the poet of the *Clef d'amors* made other versions, usually in French octosyllables. "Versions" is perhaps the right word to use; for though all of these writers can translate Ovid closely when they wish, none translates him in his entirety, but rather selects, condenses, simplifies, and adapts him to his own view of life. Each has

     THE COMEDY OF EROS

his own talents and ambitions: the simple, straight-forward Maître Élie, the concise, would-be moralistic Guiart, and the sophisticated, involuntarily anonymous author of the *Clef*, the only one to attempt all three books of the master.[6]

Ovid is not without influence on another abundant series of treatises that touch on the art of conducting a love affair: namely, those down-to-earth poems on the prudent conduct of one's life, and the proper behavior of men and women in polite society. Though all these didactic treatises tend to repeat the same ideas, they are, again, distinguished by their authors' talents and points of view. *On Courtesy* is practical and opportunistic, and seems to belong to all ages and no particular ethical system. Robert de Blois's *Advice to Ladies* plunges us into the atmosphere of the thirteenth-century *bourgeoisie*, though many of his precepts find parallels in Ovid. The reader may have his reasons to suspect that the Maître Élies and Guiarts are playing a game, but the works in this second group are surely intended seriously.

There is yet a third current of writings that we must mention. Aristotle's speculations on *philia*—the feelings that friends have for one another, feelings that may run through the whole range of emotions between loving and liking—are at the beginning of a long line of similar speculations. Cicero's *On Friendship* gives way to the Fathers on Christian friendship; the twelfth century sees Aelred of Rievaulx and Pierre de Blois writing on spiritual friendship; while Guillaume de Saint-Thierry attacks the *Ars amatoria* and makes a kind of indirect reply to it in his own treatise *On the Nature and Dignity of Love*.[7] Whether with or without a Christian intention, love and friendship had been codified and schematized by the schoolmen and the mystics. Against this background of serious thought, the work of the cleric Andreas Capellanus, *On the Art of Courtly Love* (ca. 1184/85), must seem ironic, even frivolous. Its three books—for Ovid's work is comprised of three, after all—purport to guide a young man in the ways of love. They do so first by defining love and its nature. Then, with a series of dialogues, which were to be immensely popular, they tell how to address mistresses of various social classes, and how to win their favor; they produce (by a pagan revelation) the rules of love; and, finally, the last book points out the all-round folly of involving oneself in a business devastating to the health of body and soul alike. Andreas knew an international readership and is still taken by many scholars as the supreme exponent of courtly love and its rules. In modern times, his Latin has been carefully edited and a modern English translation made, so that Andreas's fame is secure. Long ago, he had already received the accolade of a ban by the bishop of Paris and a translation into French by Drouart la Vache, a century after the appearance of his work. Drouart's verse being derivative, we offer here only a sample, the famous "Rules of Love"; enough, however, to display both the nature of Andreas's material, and the way in which the French vernacular deals with it. Andreas's influence is to be felt on Richard de Fournival, chancellor of Rheims cathedral and a far more worldly cleric than Guillaume de Saint-Thierry. In his prose *Advice on Love*, herein translated, converge the currents of school speculation, Ovid and the romances, and Andreas himself.

These texts offer a fair sample of thirteenth-century vernacular instruction in the art of love. They are, of course, only part of a long, distinguished French tradition. Without claiming to have discovered any unknown literary geniuses, one may safely say that they are a neglected facet of their times. They have had, for the most part, the misfortune of being published in inaccessible nineteenth-century German dissertations and buried in weighty philological journals. With honorable exceptions, their learned editors have not produced the best texts or the best introductions and annotations. It is to be hoped that these specimens will, at least, offer some notion as to their nature.

James B. Wadsworth

Medford, Massachusetts
September 1970

THE COMEDY OF EROS

# Ovid's "On the Art..."

## MAÎTRE ÉLIE

THE AUTHOR OF WHAT IS GENERALLY CONSIDERED the oldest surviving medieval French translation of Ovid's *Art of Love* gave his name as Maître Élie, and wrote his octosyllabic couplets in the early thirteenth century. From his text, it appears that he knew Paris, and may well have been a Parisian. Other than that, he is quite unknown. His work has come down in a single manuscript, a poorly written and seemingly unfinished copy, whose abbreviated title was probably affixed by a scribe.

Many of the characteristics of the medieval translators of Ovid are already present in Maître Élie's lines. He passes the subject off as his own ("Listen," he says, "to what I shall tell you from my own experience . . ."); he prunes out almost all of Ovid's mythological references and ornamentation; he makes no pretense of retaining the Roman atmosphere of the original, but adapts it—sometimes surprisingly well—to his own times. The Roman poet's cynical irony and amusement have gone, though we encounter a certain cynicism of Maître Élie's own. Above all, he has cut down the original relentlessly. Only Ovid's book 1 is reasonably well represented; book 2 less so; and book 3, Ovid's advice to women, remains untouched. Maître Élie's 1,305 octosyllables thus do not do full justice to the original. At times, his translation is concise and close to the text, especially when rendering the more straightforwardly didactic passages of Ovid; at other times he is unclear and pedestrian, and gives the impression of imperfect understanding of his source. He is not, in short, the best of these translators of Ovid.

Despite this judgment, there are, however, two or three passages where Maître Élie shows boldness and originality. His lines 89–150, translated here, correspond quite closely to Ovid *Ars amatoria* 1. 41 ff., except that he has adapted them to his own circumstances. His allusions to Paris, to Saint-Germain des Prés, the surrounding streets, have so natural an air that they evoke a genre picture of low-life Paris. And all the more so because it is the very things Maître Élie describes—the search for damsels walking and dancing in the neighborhood of the great abbey, the rendezvous of lovers outside the church, and even within—that the moralists of the age condemn.

The second passage translated here (Maître Élie's verses 396–442, corresponding to Ovid *Ars amatoria* 1. 397 ff.) reveals a more curious transposition of the original. Ovid advises the would-be lover to seize the favorable moment for pressing his advances: the time is not always right to set sail, to plough the fields, nor to pursue a maiden. Maître Élie sees the problem in a different light: the passionate wife will know how to take advantage of her husband's absences, the apprentice seducer will, without effort, profit from her cunning. But the official medieval mind did think of women as daughters of the devil after all.

*Text:* H. Kühne and E. Stengel, *Maître Élie's Uberarbeitung der ältesten französischen Übertragung von Ovid's Ars Amatoria* (Marburg, 1886).

### BIBLIOGRAPHICAL NOTE

Apart from the introduction to the edition of the text, and Gaston Paris's brief remarks in his chapter, "Les anciennes versions françaises de l'*Art d'aimer* et des *Remèdes d'amour* d'Ovide," in *La Poésie du moyen âge*, première série (Paris, 1885), no study of Maître Élie seems to have been made.

Now, gallant sir, when off a-wooing,
Learn where to do your best pursuing;
For as a suitor you should know
Those haunts where wenches come and go,
And where, at length, you may discover
One who will let you be her lover.
For such advice you need but ask us:
We will not send you to Damascus,
To ply your quest for womankind
In far-off lands, when you can find
Your fill of dame and damosel
Close by, in Paris! Truth to tell,
There is no land the world around
Where such a wealth of belles abound,
Much to man's joy. And every one,
Schooled in the ways of love, has done
Her lessons well; for Venus lives
Among them, one and all, and gives
Constant instruction in her art.
Would you desire to turn your heart
Toward virgin maiden, fair of feature—
Bosomless, soft and tender creature?
There is no dearth of such as these.
Or would you rather take your ease
With wench less fresh but more mature?
If so, you can be more than sure
That every sidewalk in the city
Will sport so many, pert and pretty,
That you may find yourself hard-pressed
To choose the one that suits you best.
Or if, by chance, your preference veers
Toward ladies of still fuller years—
The older, wiser kind—these too
Can well be found, and quite a few.

So take a look among the many
Who flock about, to see if any
Have what you want. "But where?" you say.
"Over by Saint-Germain des Prés."
"Why there?" you ask. And we reply
"Why there indeed! Well, this is why:
All round about the streets are laden
With many a gay, cavorting maiden
Ready to talk of love. And should
You see, midst so much maidenhood,
None you would care to have, then hie you
Right to the church, where bye and bye you
Cannot but find your pleasure. For,
There in the space before the door,
You can see pass a whole parade—
Lady and lass, madam and maid—
All with the same intent. (While some,
Certain to find their lover, come
To meet him there, the rest assume
That they will love, but don't know whom.)
So if you please the one you choose,
You may be sure she'll not refuse. . . ."
Your lady may be one of those
Who, when it comes to love, suppose
That certain times are *à propos*
And others not. Do ploughmen sow
Their fields; do sailors ply the seas,
Roaming the waves when best they please?
Not so! And thus, for love as well,
Some times are fair, some times are fell.
Though suitor craves his wench today,
She may insist that he delay,
And wait for more propitious season.
Needless to say, she has her reason:
Woman, indeed, is not so free
To come and go as man; for he
Wanders his way throughout the town—

Round and about, and up and down—
With never a fear that tongues will chatter.
For her it's quite a different matter.
Thus, when her time is ripe, and when
Something within her yearns for men,
You may be sure, she never squanders
Much time in talk, but duly ponders
Upon the place where her desire
Will find a proper satisfier.
Now, should her husband be a knight,
It stands to reason that he might
Make many a time-consuming journey—
Off to the court, off to a tourney,
Or even off to fight a war.
Thus, for a fortnight—maybe more—
The lady lives alone, and loses
No time in bidding whom she chooses
To come and keep her company.
Or does her husband chance to be
A merchant? Well, so much the better:
That gives her swain more time to get her!
For when her husband ventures forth,
Selling his wares from south to north—
Down to Apulia, or up among
Those countrymen of Frisian tongue—
Then it's at least seven months before
He can set foot inside his door!
Or is he one of the *bourgeoisie?*
No problem there; I guarantee
He will have more than ample share
Of tasks that need his constant care,
No end of everyday demands:
Now off to guard his pasturelands,
Now feed his flocks, now bring them home,
Now tend his hives of honeycomb,
Laden with bees and wax and honey.
For his concern is making money,

While her concern is making sure
To get the word to her paramour.
She sends the message; he receives it,
Flies to her side, and scarcely leaves it. . . .

MAÎTRE ÉLIE

# The Key to Love

THE *Key to Love* IS THE LONGEST, THE BEST written, and the most attractive of the medieval French retellings of Ovid's *Art of Love*. The author, a Norman, has a gift for graceful verse and does not lack imagination, charm, and wit. He also shows ingenuity, indeed excessive ingenuity. He promises at the outset to reveal his own name, his "darling, pretty lady's" name, and the date of his work; but when we reach the riddle which concludes the poem, we have to admit that it is impenetrable. One attempted reading of the riddle suggests as late a date as 1280, although a much earlier date is possible.

No less a personage than the god of love appears to the author in a dream, and orders him to compose a portable book of rules, a *portehors* or breviary which the would-be lover can carry with him at all times. The author is quite sure that his vision was authentic: do not the theologians speak of such visions, and did he not hear the rustling of the god's wings? Unlike his predecessors, whose arts of love have not pleased the god, he proposes to be brief. Indeed, he contrives to limit his adaptation of Ovid to 3,400 lines. He follows Ovid's threefold plan: the choice and finding of a mistress; the winning of her favors (physical, it goes without saying); and the continuation of this happy state. Unlike his more misogynistic competitors (though he has been touched by the same brush himself), he also presents the meat of Ovid's third book, advice to the ladies. He shows a fair originality and independence in adapting the Latin poem, shortening it, or adding

details where his tastes suggest them, at times fol-
lowing closely, almost line by line, especially in
purely didactic passages. The *Key* is shorn of Ovid's
basic metaphor—piloting the inexperienced lover
through the stormy seas of love to safe harbor—of
mythological example and almost all mythological
allusion. The verse form, octosyllabic couplets—the
favorite form of medieval narrative poetry—allows
freedom of development, however; and our poet's
rules, though clearly presented in neat packages, re-
tain the life of his model, while assuming their own
coloration. Even when he follows Ovid closely, he
adapts the Latin text to his own times, and with little
effort of the imagination one can see him as he
searches through the streets and squares, the
churches and tournament grounds of a medieval
city, rather than through the sites of ancient Rome.
And one can admire his particularly loving descrip-
tion of the dress and appearance of the *jeunesse
dorée* of his day.

Though the author of the *Key* adopts Ovid's cyn-
icism, he has his own marked preferences. He
rejects Ovid's suggestion that there is both pleasure
and profit to be found in the amorous embraces of
old women. Indeed, a desire for freshness, beauty,
youth, refinement, and elegance pervades his lines.
Without a shade of the moralist's indignation, and
with more reticence than is to be found in others of
these medieval *Arts*, he condemns the crude Don
Juans, the noisy, drunken brawlers, and so forth.
There are odd lapses: where Ovid advises sprinkling
water on the face to simulate tears, he prefers the
effects of an onion (did he mean to be serious?);
where Ovid advises picking a mistress only when
one is sober, he prefers to concentrate on the un-
happy effects of wine on the feminine complexion.
Love exists for him wholly outside of marriage:
marriage is but *sochonnerie*, "horse trading," in
which the husband is master, the wife a prisoner.
Neither the *Remedia amoris* of Ovid nor the reli-
gious attitudes of his day seem to have troubled the

serenity of his conscience or self-assurance. Though he coins, on occasion, a neat maxim, he is no moralist in the English sense of the word.

With the exception of the introductory lines, in which the poet speaks of his own beloved and of his dream, the passages translated below represent the text of the *Key* from verse 169 to verse 1296, as well as one later passage. In addition to a number of minor cuts here and there, five sizable passages have been omitted: verses 349–424, on dress and appearance; 801–96, on various precepts of behavior, etc.; 1044–84, on making and not keeping promises; 1161–1200, on a lover's perseverance; and 1221–56, on hypocritical amiability as a means to an end.

The last extract (verses 2121–66) corresponds to a passage in Ovid's third book. It is included here as an example of Ovidian advice to the ladies rare in these medieval *Arts*, but especially because it shows the awareness of the flight of time, the fragility of human beauty—the *carpe diem* thoughts only Renaissance and Cavalier poets are supposed to have entertained.

*Text:* Auguste Doutrepont, ed., *La Clef d'amors*, critical text with introduction, appendix, and glossary, Bibliotheca Normannica, vol. 5 (Halle, 1890). The *Clef d'amors* had a long and successful career: it survives in three manuscripts and, between the same covers with other Arts of Love, in three late fifteenth- and sixteenth-century editions printed in Paris, Geneva, and Antwerp, the last appearing about 1580.

BIBLIOGRAPHICAL NOTE

There appears to be no study since Doutrepont's edition. There is, however, a brief summary and appreciation in Gaston Paris, "Les anciennes versions françaises de *l'Art d'aimer* et des *Remèdes d'amour* d'Ovide," in *La Poésie du moyen âge*, première série (Paris, 1885).

This book of mine will bear the name
*The Key to Love;* for I proclaim
That with this key, one will uncover
Canons to guide the courtly lover.
But be advised, this gentle art
Is meant for those of tender heart:
Let them alone come study here.
Fie on all others—insincere
And traitorous lovers—foul and fell
Invidious souls, content to dwell
In villainy! Let them not try
To learn the laws of love hereby
Disclosed, but let them go their way!
For, strive and struggle though they may,
I fear such scurvy folk can never
Know anything of love whatever.

First learn this rule, you who would lead
A life of love: you must proceed
To choose with care and circumspection
An object worth your heart's affection.
Once you have found the maiden who
Deserves your loving, then pursue
And pay her court, as lover should,
With words to woo her maidenhood—
Sweet-sounding words to charm and flatter,
In endless flow of amorous chatter.
(Here let me not neglect to mention
Another thought worth your attention:
This love of which I speak must not
Flourish awhile, then be forgot.
It should not be but briefly tried,
Soon to be scorned and cast aside:
Who loves tonight and leaves tomorrow

Turns joy to grief and cheer to sorrow.)
Now, if you wonder how and where
A man may find his lady fair,
Listen, as I set forth below
The things I think you need to know.

As long as you can go and come
Footloose and free, *ad libitum*,
If you should feel yourself inclined
To loving, wait until you find
A lass to whom you can protest:
"Milady, more than all the rest
Of womankind, I yearn for you!"
Now, *à propos* and thereunto,
Learn where to look when you are seeking
This love of which we have been speaking:
Try not to roam too far afield,
Lest your intentions be revealed
To one and all; for—never doubt—
Love spreads its presence roundabout.
And when one sees a gallant youth
In far-flung places where, in truth,
He has no proper need to dwell,
One knows his heart is there as well:
A distant love moves tongues to prattle,
And gives the gossips tales to tattle.
But if, withal, you still decide
To do your loving far and wide,
Look for a true and faithful friend
Close by; then you may well pretend
That all those visits you will make
Are merely for his friendship's sake.

Now that you know where I suggest
You go to ply the lover's quest,
Next in our lesson we shall pass
From *where* to *when* you woo the lass.

*The Key to Love*

13

When man would choose his heart's delight,
Let him not trust the dark of night.
For, as I oftentimes maintain,
In darkness chaff will pass for grain:
However brightly burns the wick,
The candlelight plays many a trick.
Thus, he who woos by night cannot
Ever be sure what he has caught.
And so, by right, let him take care
Lest fair seem foul, and foul seem fair!
Another thought well worth the thinking:
Beware the lady lately drinking;
Whatever truth the wine exposes,
It hides much more than it discloses.
For, though it moves her tongue apace,
Wine hides the truth of woman's face:
Even if she is full of wrinkles,
Furrowed with crow's-feet, cracks and crinkles,
Wine stirs the blood within the veins
And swells them till her face regains
The flush of youthful loveliness,
However pale and colorless
It may, alas, have grown. And so,
I should advise the would-be beau
That he had best be disinclined
To woo the woman too well wined:
Be sure to do your courting first,
Before the wench has quenched her thirst!

Now, you have heard and understood
Both where and when I think you should
Engage in amorous endeavor.
I have not yet described, however,
Whom you must seek in your pursuits,
And what should be her attributes:
She must be simple, sweet and fresh,
Tender of years and fair of flesh,

Unspoiled of manner, mien and mood,
Of candid, courtly attitude.
(Or if, indeed, a more mature,
Somewhat more seasoned paramour
Is what you chance to have in mind,
Let me assure you, man will find
His fill of those to choose among:
The old ones far exceed the young!)
If you are wise, then pay your court
In circles of the noblest sort,
Where, if you will, you may select
A woman worth the world's respect,
Of proper birth and pedigree:
The higher a lady's family tree,
The more is she disposed to do
What you and Nature want her to;
Whereas the lass of lowly station
Requires far more solicitation.
Thus I would urge you, when you love,
Shun those below for those above.
Then boldly take the one you choose:
No well-bred lady will refuse
To ease a loyal lover's anguish;
She pities all who pine and languish!
(Indeed, the lady who denies
Her solace to the soulful sighs
Of earnest lover, courting duly,
Is not, I fear, a lady truly:
She is, despite her gentle birth
And noble rank, of humble worth.
Be quick to curb love's tender leaning
For one so proudly overweening;
Because, for all her high degree,
You may be sure, no lady she!)
Some timid hearts there are, who shrink
From highborn ladies, prone to think
That their attentions may displease.

Never, I pray, be one of these;
For Ovid states with certitude
That any woman rightly wooed
In properly befitting fashion
Will not deny love's gentle passion.
His words should make you bold enough
To woo and win despite rebuff.
For any woman's heart will yield
To love respectfully revealed;
And willingly will she surrender
To man whose suit is sweet and tender.
In short, when all is said and done,
Every woman can be won:
Let any gallant come pursue her,
Her flattered pride will soon undo her.

At this point I have taught you who
The women are that you may woo.
Next I should like to turn my thought
To you yourself, and how you ought
Not fail to act, if your pursuit
Of passion is to bear you fruit.
Above all, strive to learn discretion;
For common sense and self-possession
Adorn man more than comeliness.
His beauty goes for naught, unless
Within his favored form there dwell
Wisdom and worldly wit as well:
Fair though the unwise man may be,
He is but lifeless effigy!
Be courteous, courtly, *comme il faut*,
From top of head to tip of toe:
A life of high esteem demands
Both open heart and open hands.
Withal, be smooth and glib of tongue,
No matter whom you move among:
Those flattering phrases, tried and true,

ANONYMOUS

Cost lovers little, *entre nous*.
Beware, as well, lest lofty pride
Prompt you to deeds undignified:
Some coarse and vulgar men resort
To acts of force when love falls short;
Such men as these do not deserve
The ladies they pretend to serve.
Love will not yield to man's beseeching
If he is rude and overreaching:
From haughty heights man well may fall
To deep despair, beyond recall;
But let him woo in humble guise,
Then all the higher will he rise.
And yet, despite your modest air,
Never be loath to do and dare,
As deft and doughty gallant must.
For cowardice begets disgust;
And timid suitor—meek, unmanned—
Will win no lady's heart or hand.

The rules hereinabove expressed
Should be engraved within your breast.
Now, if you truly wish to learn
The lover's art, then let us turn
To yet another consequential
Lesson in love, a most essential
Subject for your concern: to wit,
Your body and how to care for it.
First let me speak about the hair
To hopeful suitors everywhere:
I do insist that you attempt
Always to keep it clean and kempt;
While you who are more sparsely topped
May well prefer it closely cropped.
(One thing is sure: short locks or long,
To wear a wig is clearly wrong!)
Then too, if you are one of those

With bristles sprouting from the nose,
Or if the hairs grow long and thick
Between the brows, go pluck them quick!
As for the care of eye and ear,
The love-intentioned cavalier
Must keep the former and the latter
Free of all foul, offensive matter.
You must, as well, strive day and night
To keep your teeth spotless and white,
With mouth as pure as mouth can be,
Cleansed of all vile impurity,
Lest, when you go to woo the wench,
Your breath offend with fetid stench.
Another rule of *politesse:*
Your face had best go whiskerless;
Be sure to have it plucked or shaved
By one whose hand is well behaved,
And who will do it to perfection.
As for the care of your complexion,
Beware: some thoughtless men bewail
A lip too white, a cheek too pale.
If you are prone to such complaint,
Pray shun the use of tint and paint,
Which many wear who, vainly, try
To better Nature's work thereby.
For Nature knows what she is doing;
And when a lover goes pursuing,
He must not seem too hale, too fit,
But rather quite the opposite—
Pallid and frail and gaunt—to show
How harshly love has laid him low:
No swain by heart's travail possessed
Looks plump and sleek and pleasure-blessed.
Pale, haggard cheeks bespeak the spending
Of sleepless, yearning nights unending—
Nights that all tender suitors pass,
Learning to sigh: "Alack, alas!" . . .

ANONYMOUS

You must, in truth, seize every chance,
Every seemly circumstance,
To meet your lady face to face.
Does she frequent the market place?
Then you should hie and hasten there!
For people swarm from everywhere,
Moving about in bustling throng.
At length she too will come along;
And then, should you desire, you may
Take her aside and have your say.
Is she, perchance, a churchly lass?
Then seek her out at Holy Mass:
Amid the multitude of people—
Somewhere betwixt the crypt and steeple—
It should not be too hard to find
A spot where you may speak your mind.
Many another place will do,
As well, for amorous rendezvous:
At rustic roundelay and *fête*,
Tripping to flute and flageolet,
You may—while prancing to and fro—
Tell her what you would have her know.
(Or, at the least, though feet be dancing,
Your eyes can speak with tender glancing!)
You can, as well, set out your snare
Along the open thoroughfare,
About those booths where jugglers stand,
Showing their feats and sleights of hand.
Then too, those tourneys—noble sport,
Where knights cross steel for king and court,
Pitting their skill with manly pride—
Those tourneys, I repeat, provide
A fitting field for you who would
Learn the delights of womanhood.
For many a fancy wench abounds
Round and about the tilting grounds;
Gaily they flock from far and near.

*The Key to Love*                                    19

(Though less intent to see, I fear,
Than to be seen and amply eyed!)
And so, one day, should it betide
That king and suite, on royal journey,
Ride into town to hold a tourney,
Go to the lists and you will spy
The one you long for, bye and bye.
Wait in the stands; or, if you will,
Watch from behind a window sill.
Your presence there need not provoke
The prattling tongues of tattling folk:
All kinds of people come to view
This knightly sport, so why not you?
When she appears, go down to greet her:
Contrive to wait where you must meet her,
Edging as close as it behooves.
With hidden glance and subtle moves—
Lest others fathom what is meant—
Make known to her your heart's intent.
Such is the start of your amour.
Next, when you go to speak, be sure
To rattle on with trifling chatter,
Talking of things that little matter,
In language plain and commonplace:
"Whose steeds come trotting here apace?...
And whose are those?... And whose are
    these?..."
Whatever answer it may please
The lady to propose, I pray
You voice an "aye" and not a "nay."
Never deny, distrust or doubt
Anything she holds forth about.
(At least, she must not think you do!)
Does she sing praises? Sing them too.
Does she speak ill, and chide, and slur?
Needless to say, you must concur.
Indeed, though arrantly absurd,

ANONYMOUS

Hang on the lady's every word;
For, though she spout inanities,
Woman affirms...and man agrees!
Have specks of dust or bits of dirt
Fallen upon her cloak or skirt?
Go to her side and linger there,
Plucking them off with studied care.
(And even if he should see no dust,
The nimble-witted suitor must
Pretend to spy some none the less,
Brushing it gently from her dress.)
Seize every chance that happens by,
To pamper, please and satisfy.
Is she, perhaps, so fully gowned
That skirt falls trailing to the ground?
Go lift it just a trifle higher
Out of the nasty muck and mire.
(For lady, gallantly pursued,
Repays a man's solicitude;
Let him but dote, as suitor ought:
Soon he will have what he has sought.)
And when, at length, you take your seat,
Shield her from tread of trampling feet.
Be on your guard, as well, to soften
Those jostling jolts that, all too often,
Come from the people sitting near.
In short, my courtly cavalier,
Be wise and serve your lady best;
For nothing sways her fickle breast
Like thoughtful little gallantries—
Tender attentions such as these.
And when the kings and counts ride through
With all their royal retinue,
And when the barons, stoutly steeled,
Bestride their mounts and take the field,
The lady may be moved to say:
"Pray tell me sire, what men are they?"


*The Key to Love*

Be positive when you reply,
Without so much as "what?" or "why?"—
Pretending (if you do not know)
That one is king of So-and-so,
And one is count of You-know-where:
"Ah yes, fair lady, that one there
Comes all the way from Chartres town;
While that one riding farther down
Has his domains in Île-de-France."
Now, if you know their names, by chance,
Announce them loud and clear; if not,
Invent some good ones on the spot.
And if she never asks a name?
No matter: tell her all the same.
For I would have all lovers learn
Not to be cold and taciturn:
Let him whose lips possess the skill
Of pleasing speech go speak his fill.
Cordial, congenial intercourse
Is oftentimes the very source
Of those sweet feelings that impart
Love's arrow-pangs to mind and heart.

Some evening it may well betide
That you will find yourself beside
The lady of your choice at table.
If so, you should be more than able
To seize a chance when you and she
May chat together, *vis-à-vis*.
For dining time is, after all,
Given to festive folderol,
When every guest will chaff and twit,
To show the rest his restless wit;
When wine—that carefree foe of sadness—
Moves one and all to games of gladness
And revelries of every sort.
Amid this mirth and sprightly sport

You would do well, I might suggest,
To be your gallant, gracious best:
Passions conceived in such condition
Most often yield a full fruition.

In all my teachings hitherto,
I have revealed the how, the who,
The where, the when of courtly wooing.
At this point, in the lines ensuing,
Let me explain by what devices
The suitor, deftly taught, entices
That lady whom his love demands,
Until her heart lies in his hands.
With confidence you must begin,
Firm in the hope that you will win:
However rich, however fair,
There is no maiden anywhere
Who, when a young and gentle lad
Pays her his court, cannot be had!
For sooner would the birds fall mute
And hounds neglect the hare's pursuit
Than would a woman's heart reject
A lover courteous and correct.
Even the sanctimonious prude,
All rigid, righteous rectitude—
The one you look to last of all—
Often will be the first to fall.
(Though such may claim that they eschew it,
We know how game they are to do it!)
So well has Love—our teacher—taught,
That each of us, at length, is brought
To be his eager devotee.
(God knows what feeble creatures we!)
Indeed, both man and woman bend
The knee before him in the end,
Happy to heed his beck and call.
Yet differences exist, withal;

*The Key to Love*

For man and woman do not use
The same devices: man pursues,
And importunes, and prays, and pleads;
While woman slyly, coyly leads
Her lover on. (Of course, she may,
In time, have cause herself to pray
And plead to him with heartfelt yearning:
Love's tables have a way of turning!)
Ladies who answer naught but no
To every good and gallant beau
Commit a wrongful, woeful act
At odds with Nature; for, in fact,
It is demanded by the latter
That love shall be the only matter
Ever to move their hearts to caring.
Therefore, young man, be bold, be daring:
Ply them with passion unrepressed;
For, though their fickle mouths protest,
Rare is the woman who does not
Delight to see herself besought.
And so, press on and on, despite
Refusals cold and impolite.
Such is the woman's native bent
That, though she burn with one intent,
Still she will make man pine and pray
Before her eager heart gives way,
Fearing he might esteem her less
Were she too quick to acquiesce.

Next let me say that, if you trust
My teaching and advice, you must
Leave no resources unessayed
To make the lady's chambermaid—
The one to whom she bares her breast—
Consent to serve your interest.
She is the one most sure to know
How well or ill your suit will go

And what your wooing may beget.
So, work to wheedle her soubrette;
For when you win her to your side,
You will, indeed, be well allied.
She knows her mistress' moods; thus shall you
Find her advice of signal value,
Since she can counsel you, with reason,
Which is the properest time and season
To sue the lady and succeed.
Often a woman pays no heed
At all to passion—not a whit—
While other times she yearns for it:
As with all things, there is a moment
Most opportune for love's bestowment.
(Of the four seasons, one above
The rest stands out as best for love:
Those gay, green, sprightly days of spring,
Season of sweet awakening,
When woman's merry moods transport her—
Such is a seemly time to court her!)
And if it happens—as it might—
That she know bitter, dark despite
Because her lover casts her out
To take another, she may pout
And wail and weep a while—so be it:
She can be yours, I guarantee it!
The true and trusted chambermaid,
At such a moment, may persuade
Her mistress' mind in myriad ways,
Serving your cause with words of praise.
The lady will be duly awed
When, thus, the maid sees fit to laud
Your goodly worth and courtliness
In language fraught with *gentillesse:*
"This lad is gentle, worldly-wise,
Tidy and trim in outward guise,
A jovial fellow through and through—

*The Key to Love*

Just the right age for such as you.
Look high and low, afar and near:
I know you will not find his peer,
No matter where you chance to seek.
He is a man of worth unique,
A youth deserving (more than many)
Of lady's favors—all or any—
And one who now, in truth, would fain
Become your loyal, loving swain.
For you he sobs his plaintive sighs:
Oh, how his heart must agonize,
Caught in the woe your charm has wrought!
I pray, dear lady, ease his lot:
Let him but love and cherish you,
As gentle suitor longs to do.
Naught but delight and joy can come
To lover and his lass therefrom;
For no one knows what bliss can be
Who has not served Love's seigniory.
And so, Milady, why delay?
Go love the lad while love you may:
Those who spurn tender passion, till
It seems to suit their own sweet will,
Discover, when their minds are set,
That what they want they cannot get!"
With these or other such-like phrases
The lady's maid will sing your praises
Until, in time, the heretofore
Unwilling wench says nay no more.
So use the maid as I suggest,
For woman hoodwinks woman best.

Such is the role that may be played
By love-abetting chambermaid.
Only beware, lest you be led
By lust to bring her to your bed,
There to seduce and sleep with her.

ANONYMOUS

For once you touch the maid, you err
In your endeavors amatory,
And mar your chances, *a priori:*
The maid, much moved, will never let you
Out of her sight, but will beset you,
Striving by day and night to make
Your mind forget, your heart forsake
The lady lately coveted,
To keep you for herself instead.
And if her mistress ever learned
That, from her wooing, you had turned
To love her chambermaid, I vow
She would not have you anyhow!
For but one hour of lustfulness
You will, alas, lie ladyless!
And thus, the canny swain and clever,
Bent on success in love's endeavor,
Must be intent, in his amours,
Not to make random overtures
Round and about. He had far better
Choose whom he wants...and then go get her!

Next must the suitor, passion plighting,
Master the art of letter-writing.
Therefore, if you should wish to woo,
Learn how to turn those *billets doux*
That humbly, sweetly bare the soul—
Whether it be on parchment scroll
Or waxen tablet, little matter,
So long as you cajole and flatter,
Over and over, unrelenting.
However cold and unconsenting
The lady may at first appear,
Still must you press and persevere;
For passionate, persistent wooing
Will prove the hardest heart's undoing. . . .
And so, be sure to learn the style

*The Key to Love*

That will, in proper wise, beguile
Your winsome woman: spurn the use
Of brutish words that might produce
A rude and unrefined effect;
Use, rather, those that will reflect
Your gallant, gentle predilection—
Then will you earn her fond affection.
Be certain, too, when thus you write,
Not to commit the oversight
Of mentioning her name therein—
Or even yours: naught but chagrin
Would come of it if gossips found
Your names, and spread the news around,
Much to your love's discomfiture;
For love laid bare cannot endure.
No harder pain can be imposed
Than when one's passion lies disclosed:
Tattlers will point and poke their fun,
Till love grows weak and comes undone.
Wherefore, beware: write letters, yes—
But as for names, just let them guess!
Folly it is to bare, unbidden,
What best would be withheld and hidden.
And now, another necessary
Rule for pursuit epistolary:
Promise her gifts—and not a few!—
Worth, one and all, a pretty sou.
(The gallant lad who knows this rule
And works it well is no one's fool!)
For promises can do no harm,
But, rather, titillate and charm
The lady's tender disposition.
However paltry man's condition,
Fine promises are lavished free.
He cannot keep them?... Ah, *tant pis!*
Promise galore: it will astound you
How fast the ladies flock around you,

All hanging on your doublet strings,
Hoping to have those lovely things
That ladies long and hunger for.
Well, make them linger evermore:
Young hearts and old, sick minds and sane
Yield to the hope of worldly gain.
As their desire for wealth grows stronger,
Feign that they need not wait much longer;
But never, I implore you, should
You give them what you said you would.
Offer them naught but words to whet
Their lust for gifts they shall not get.
For this is how most women are:
They take your gifts...then *au revoir!* . . .
And if the lady whom man chooses
Rejects his letter, and refuses
Even to read, "What then?" you ask.
Indeed, the hopeful suitor's task
Is made more difficult thereby;
Still, you must never cease to try.
For she will soon be sorrow-smitten
Not to have read what you had written;
Whatever woman's mind may think,
It turns about in but a twink!
So, if today she spurns your letter,
Write on: anon she will do better.
Now, it may happen that, instead
Of leaving what you write unread,
She may, in fact, see fit to read it,
And yet be ill disposed to heed it.
In such a case it is not wise
To chide, deplore or criticize
The lady who makes no reply.
Write all the more; for bye and bye
She will be moved to make response—
Though I must add that, for the nonce,
You may not find her answer very

Loving, or like to make you merry.
In first replying, *au contraire*,
She will assume a solemn air—
Sullen and stern—and she will pray
You cease your suit and go your way,
Never to dare pursue her more.
Needless to say, you must ignore
Such admonition and reproof.
For, though she shout from every roof
That she will never have you, still,
After a while she surely will!
Though staunch and steadfast her insistence,
You can have done with her resistance.
A lady's nay is mere device
To see if man will ask her twice! . . .
And so, persist: the woodman's axe
Must toil before the tree trunk cracks.
Remember, too, how well Ulysses
Wheedled those Carthaginian misses: [8]
Though far from fair, he soon unstrung them,
And made the noblest ones among them
Yield to his will—so goes the story—
With smooth and sweet-tongued oratory.
Thus, in your letters, try to let
Love's language aid your *amourette*,
With words that spur (though sweet and
    gentle)—
Persuasive words, yet sentimental.
And so, may artful pen express
What absent tongue would fain profess. . . .

At table, when the wine flows free,
A man must mind his dignity.
He should not quaff and tipple till
His face bespeaks his belly's fill,
Or guzzle down the trellis-juice
Till head and foot forget their use.

ANONYMOUS

Nor let him quarrel, carp and shout,
Lest he be thought a lowly lout.
Such boorish manners ill befit
The well-bred man of worth and wit:
None but the base, beshitten troop
Will brawl and bicker, yelp and whoop.
And so, I pray you never let
The cup betray good etiquette
By making you commit, unthinking,
Those brutish acts brought on by drinking.
(Yet you need not sit still and dumb,
Immutable and mutely mum.
Much may you do that will not breach
Rules of good taste in deed and speech:
You may sing songs—if you are able—
Or jovially regale the table
With witty tale and *jeu d'esprit.*)
At length, amid the revelry,
A water basin will be placed
Before the spattered, greasy-faced
And fatty-fingered guests there sitting.
At such a time it would be fitting
To take your lady by the hand,
Conduct her to the washing stand,
And let her be the first to dip
Therein her dainty finger tip.
While thus you touch her flesh, dissemble:
Pretend your heart is all a-tremble,
Burning with passion-fire, full-blown,
To capture for your very own
Her comely body, which your eyes
Devour—nay, fairly gormandize!
No lady doubts that she inspires
A lover's heart with such desires;
And thus, this passionate pretense
Will have its proper recompense:
It will—as I have often found—

Wear down the wench and bring her round.
Learn this as well: some men are much
Too bold and brash, and love to touch
The lady's tender toes with theirs.
Are you of such a sort that dares
Indulge in undertable banter?
Well, you may rue the day *instanter*.
Another's foot may be there, lurking,
Bent and intent on mischief-working,
Waiting between her foot and yours
To catch those silent overtures
Of toe to toe. And so, beware:
A reckless foot can lay you bare
And, in a trice, make manifest
What just before was merely guessed.
(Needless to say, your foot may be
Pressed against hers as carelessly
And freely as you wish, providing
No other prying foot lies hiding.)
Therefore, I pray you, be discreet:
Spies are afoot...so mind your feet!
Now, when at length the meal is done,
The tables cleared, and everyone
Rises to leave, go join the throng;
And as you press and inch along,
Close to her side, a breath away,
Let hand and finger idly stray
Over her body, here and there.
Nor let your eager foot forbear
To mark its gentle tread on hers,
Till you are certain she infers
That you are serving love's command.
The lady may stop short, and stand
Angrily by, berating you
In terms you cannot misconstrue:
"Good sir, enough! Now get you gone!"—
Or others like them—whereupon,

Trembling before her glare and glower,
You will pretend to cringe and cower
(If you are wise) and you will beat
A most obedient, meek retreat.
For keep in mind, my cavalier:
Love is not love that knows no fear.
Thus, if you let the lady think
That she can make you quake and shrink
By word or deed, all well and good:
No doubt you love as lover should.

Here is another clever ruse.
Should ever hand or tongue refuse
To mind good taste, do like some lovers:
Feign to be drunk; for drinking covers
A multitude of sins, and so
Pardons your vulgar *gestes* and *mots*.
When man behaves like arrant sot,
The drink is blamed; the drinker, not.

Next we must put our minds to yet
Another question: whom to let
Serve as the loyal emissary
Of your amour. Be wise and wary:
Never entrust a task like this
To man, or it may go amiss.
(I know, for oftentimes have I
Seen my own wooing gone awry!)
The reasons are not hard to find:
How many a lady would unbind
Her bosom-thoughts to manly view
And speak her mind? A paltry few!
Woman trusts in her sex alone;
To man her heart is never known.
Thus, when you want your lady friend
To have your gallant message, send
Another woman—not a man—

*The Key to Love*                                    33

As go-between. For women can
Approach each other when they please;
While men are often ill at ease
In company of lady fair,
And so will sooner flee than dare
Address her face to face. Then too,
Some men are scoundrels, and will woo
Your lady for themselves, with never
Quiver of conscience whatsoever.
The Devil take such traitorous, mean,
Discourteous men, who "come between
The bowstring and the bow," delighting,
With knavish glee, in disuniting
Lover and lady—lackaday!
Cursed be their work, and cursed be they! . . .

A courtly lover must, as well,
Be glib of tongue, and must excel
At flattering phrase and epithet:
"I pray, fair-favored lady, let
My eyes but gaze their fill upon
Your wondrous face, lest—woebegone,
Hapless and hopeless—I be left
At length to languish, life-bereft."
Next, praise her eyes, her shapely nose,
Her smiling lips the tint of rose—
Of flawless form and seemly size—
And let her hear how much you prize
The comely teeth arrayed therein.
Extol her fine and well-turned chin;
Then, when you reach the neck, declare
That you lie caught within the snare
Set by its loveliness. In short,
To pay the lady proper court
You must praise everything in sight:
Tell her how fair her form, how white
Her graceful-fingered hands, how neat

And nicely kept her dainty feet.
Nor is that all. You must be quick
To turn your artful rhetoric
And all your flattering eloquence
Upon her wit, her common sense,
Her courteous air and courtly bearing.
Be no less lavish and unsparing
In praise of all her virtues, given
(So you will say) by generous Heaven.
Ply her with such applause, and she
Will have you for her *bel ami*.
Nothing a lover does can stir
A lady's heart or gladden her
As much as honeyed words, I warrant.
Does she find coquetry abhorrent?
Well, pay no mind. You may be sure
Even the chastest and most pure
Will lend a willing ear (and more)
To men who fawn and flatter; for,
Breathes there a woman anywhere
Who would not fain be passing fair?
Indeed, not so! It follows, clearly,
That any hopeful swain need merely
Utter this cry: "O beauteous one!"
No sooner will his tongue have done
Than any woman thus addressed—
Lady or lass—will yield her breast.
Even the most unsightly creature,
Shapeless of form and foul of feature,
Fancies herself a comely miss
Thanks to man's flattering artifice.
Wherefore, be wise: it well behooves you
To praise the maid when passion moves you. . . .

It would, no less, be quite in keeping
For man to learn the art of weeping
And cultivate its proper use.

*The Key to Love* 35

Yes, let your tears burst forth, profuse:
The lady sued—nay, supplicated—
With tearful torrents, unabated,
Will not stand by unmoved and cold,
Nor will she very long withhold
Her heart's compassion; for she knows
The grace that tenderness bestows
Upon a lady.  So I say,
Go make your lachrymose display,
And you will find her more than willing
To dry the tears your eyes are spilling!
"But what," you ask, "if tears refuse
To flow at will?" Well, then you use
Man's surest cure for tearless eye—
A bit of onion held close by!
Or, should you fear lest, with its stench,
It cause the lady fair to blench,
Droplets of water, deftly flecked,
Will give you quite the same effect.
In any case, when moist his cheeks,
Man always wins the one he seeks.

If you should find yourself alone
With her whom you would make your own,
Take full advantage, gallant sir,
And spare no pains in pleasing her.
Above all, lest you seem remiss,
Press her with many a burning kiss,
Seizing the chance to fill her ear
With words all ladies long to hear.
Now, should she fail to acquiesce,
Spurning your lips, your soft caress,
Your warm embrace, "What then?" you say.
Well, hug and kiss her anyway!
(Though when you do, you must, of course,
Be careful not to use such force
That she, indeed, be made to suffer:

ANONYMOUS

A wrested kiss need be no rougher
Than those she proffers uncompelled.)
At length, her flesh—too long withheld—
Will feel the pangs of love awaken,
Roused by that kiss, though brusquely taken.
For kisses are, in modest measure,
Harbingers of still greater pleasure.
And thus it may be rightly reckoned:
Who takes the first soon gets the second.

Once you have pressed your lips to hers
(Despite her long and loud demurs),
You must not stop at mere embrace:
Push on, pursue the rest apace.
What crass affront, what foul offense
To leave the lass in cruel suspense!
Love is no trifling game, intended
But to commence and then be ended;
And he who proves himself unwilling
To forge ahead toward love's fulfilling
Does not deserve—boor that he is—
To know the joys that might be his.
Of course, the lady may, perchance,
Seem to reject your rash advance,
Commanding—though her lips were kissed—
That you shall straightway cease, desist
And call a halt! But though she act
Haughty and harsh, in point of fact
She really hopes that you ignore
Her protests and persist the more,
Forcing her feeble flesh until
Love lays her low "against her will"!
(For never would her lips admit
That all her qualms are counterfeit,
And that, in spite of sigh and tear,
She prays you boldly persevere.)
So let her weep and whimper "rape!":

*The Key to Love*

37

I warrant she would not escape
Even if she were able to.
No, no! She loves that derring-do
Of brazen cavalier, undaunted.
She would feel hurt, unloved, unwanted
Were you to leave her there, forsaking
What you might have just for the taking. . . .
Well, will you falter? Not a jot!
Go to it, love her on the spot:
Despite the prudish pose she flaunts,
Give her what every woman wants! . . .

Here let me counsel special care
Lest you would see your love affair
Come to a most untimely end.
Beware the "boon and bosom friend";
Today, though he be tried and true,
Tonight he may be trying too!
For, when you sing your lady's praise
To him, will he not look for ways
To win her for himself? A stranger
Offers a lover no such danger;
But friends can do more harm than good!
Of course, it will be understood
That, even so, a suitor must
Have one companion he can trust,
And who—however grave and grim
The lover's woe—can comfort him.
A friend like this is worth much more
Than worldly wealth and gold galore.
Only remember: folly it is
To test that faithfulness of his;
So trust him, yes...but, all the same,
Never reveal the lady's name! . . .

A lover may, alas, ignore
The several rules hereinbefore

ANONYMOUS

*The Key to Love*

Set down: though they, indeed, are many,
He can refrain from heeding any
So long as he is rich. Ah, yes—
His hands can buy his heart's success!
He need not learn my art, for he
Has but to give unsparingly.
Then will he find—however crass,
Crude and ill bred—that many a lass
(And lady, too) will fairly run
To fling herself at such a one.
For let him but put hand to purse:
Then, be he blackamoor, or worse—
Barbarous, blunt Hungarian, or
Fell infidel of Aigremore [9]—
See how they fawn and fall about him!
As for the pauper, watch them flout him!
They call the poor man "dolt" and "fool,"
And flay him with harsh ridicule.
Such ladies' passion burns unceasing—
So long as man is fit for fleecing!
But once his fortune falls awry,
Oh, what a cold and quick good-by:
Let the vile creature go his way
And beg his bread as best he may!
What comfort can there be, what pleasure,
For women who will take their leisure
Toying with love for worldly gain?
Ladies of gentle worth disdain
A lover's gifts; their hearts are won,
Rather, by what is said and done
In gallant guise, than by the rich
And precious offerings for which
Those common wenches can be had.
So, ladies, love the courteous lad:
However little he may possess,
Yet what a wealth of courtliness!
His worth is not some paltry pawn

Of Fortune, proffered, then withdrawn.
No: you who love as ladies should
Will love him for his knightlihood,
Whose lofty virtues far outmeasure
And long outlast mere transient treasure. . . .

While youth is yours, Madame, I pray
You love as much as love you may.
Remember, not one day goes by
But that old age casts threatening eye
Upon your youth, intent to take it:
Go make love while you yet can make it.
For time is like the river, going
Down to the sea, and ever flowing
Onward in unrelenting course.
Thus woman must be mad, perforce,
Who waits and waits to love, until
She grows too old—as soon she will.
So use your youth, for love intended,
Lest all too quickly it be ended:
Life's after years are nevermore
As good as those that went before!
And so, while wit and beauty flower,
Fair in the newness of their hour,
Listen to Nature's call, and do
Everything she commands you to.
For you who greet with haughty "nay"
All who would pay you court today,
Will wish tomorrow—mark my word—
That you had loved and not demurred.
Then will you lie, a witless crone,
Cold in your nightly bed, alone.
No more those serenades of praise;
No more those heaps of rose-bouquets
Placed on your doorstep; nay, no more
Those swains to batter down your door.
With wrinkled face and features jaded,

*The Key to Love*

You will find all your freshness faded,
And tresses that were once of gold,
Grown ugly, dull and hoary-old.
The aging stag—so goes the fable—
By eating serpent flesh is able
Thus to regain the grace once his.[10]
Alas! I fear his method is
Of little use to such as you!
Be wise, love now, while life is new:
For beauty gone is fled forever;
Try though you may, canny and clever,
It will be lost beyond recall.
Unplucked, the flower will fade and fall.
Proud mistresses, why must you try
To best the goddesses on high?
They never saw their charms go wasted,
Nor left the joys of love untasted.
Neither should you. Come, there is ample
Good to be gained from their example. . . .

ANONYMOUS

# The Art of Love

## GUIART

THE *Art of Love* WHICH GUIART ADAPTED FROM
Ovid is notable for two reasons: unlike Maître
Élie's version or *The Key to Love*, Guiart
offers lessons from the *Remedia amoris* as well as
from the *Ars amatoria;* and secondly, he uses the
Ovidian material ostensibly only to condemn it.
Guiart himself is no more than a name to us, a man
writing in the language of the thirteenth-century
Île de France.

The sixty-four quatrains of alexandrines fall
neatly into four groups: 1–7, a preface; 8–27, the
art of winning a mistress; 28–43, how to disentangle
oneself from an affair; and finally, 44–64, a demon-
stration of the vanity of this world, how to save
one's soul, and a final invocation of the Virgin.
Needless to say, the Ovidian material is supposed to
have shown the wretchedness of life in this world,
where, for a little fleeting pleasure, men lose God
and his Mother. These last quatrains, almost a third
of the poem, thus prescribe Guiart's true remedy
for human love. And thus he has contrived to bring
together in one poem two poles of medieval think-
ing—the delights of the flesh and the horror of the
flesh.

In so brief a space, Guiart can do little more than
give a series of precepts. These concise summaries
of Ovid's doctrines, shorn of the literary garb in
which the Roman poet has clad them, are reduced
to the barest essentials, almost, at times, to proverbial
expressions which recall the style of the compilers
of vernacular wisdom-verse. Occasional scriptural
allusions ("No man can serve two masters . . . or

*The Art of Love*

two mistresses") contribute to the particular tone of the poem, half profane, half moralistic. At the same time, the speech that he puts into the suitor's mouth —so characteristic of these medieval *Arts*—recalls contemporary love poetry rather than Ovid. But Ovid surely sanctions the suitor's aim, forcible sexual conquest, even if he would be astonished at the result: marriage, pleasing to God and men, granted, of course, that the woman—not the man—be worthy.

Because of Guiart's moral side, his editor, Louis Karl, feels able to sum up as follows: "While he does not deserve the name of great poet, he is a man worthy of respect."

*Text:* The translation, which is complete except for the last fifteen stanzas, is based on the edition by Louis Karl, *Zeitschrift für romanische Philologie* 45 (1924): 66–80, 181–87.

BIBLIOGRAPHICAL NOTE

Karl's introduction is the most recent study of Guiart.

If you would learn the art of love in such a way
That none might doubt or scorn your talents,
   then I pray
You heed these rhymes so closely that, in turn,
   you may
Reveal to other would-be lovers what they say.

Master Guiart, who writes of love in common
   speech,
Will treat three subjects. First, he will attempt to
   teach
How you must undertake correctly to beseech
A lady's heart, and bring her love within your
   reach.

Next, he will try to show the path you must
   pursue
When you have won her heart; and, lastly, what
   to do
Once the fair lady's charm no longer pleases you,
And when, at length, you wish to bid her love
   adieu.

If there be some who choose to scold and censure
   me
Because they think that good and evil should not
   be
Set forth together, both in common company,
They reason ill, as I shall teach them presently.

The man who tills the soil, who ploughs and
   plants and sows,
Must first uproot the thorns and brambles, if his
   rows

*The Art of Love*

Of seedlings are to sprout. For this he surely
  knows:
The earth must be prepared, else nothing useful
  grows.

In Aristotle's book,[11] he shows how "clerics" use
All kinds of cunning craft when they wish to
  abuse
Their ladies. But he hopes, thereby, to help us
  choose
An upright life, untouched by such deceit and
  ruse.

Likewise I too shall strive, at first, to represent
The falseness of this world, on idle folly bent.
Then, lastly, I shall prove that life, in truth, is
  meant
To serve God's majesty, and in His grace be
  spent.

First you must learn to bare your wretchedness
  before
The damsel: "Maiden fair, my heart is sick and
  sore
For love of you, alas! Sweet maiden, I implore,
Love me or I shall die. I can do nothing more!

Good lady, hear your liege. Sweet sovereign, I
  confess,
My body and my heart and all that I possess
Are yours: you are my hope, my love, my life!
  Unless
You soothe and comfort me, I perish in distress.

Alas! Could you but know how keenly I have
  sought

Your love, above all else, then surely you would
  not
Deny your heart to one who has, in every
  thought,
Held you more dear each day, as loyal lover
  ought.

I tremble, yet I burn. Endlessly I complain
And sigh and moan. I try to eat and sleep: in
  vain!
No one can find a cure that might allay my pain.
Fair lady, you alone can make me well again.

Milady, comely, kind, men praise your virtues
  so—
Your faithful heart, your wit, your grace—that
  I well know
To die for love of you would be a welcome woe,
More fair than all the wealth another might
  bestow."

Now then, when she has heard you moan and
  plead and sigh,
Do not lose heart too soon if she, with scornful
  eye,
Ignores your pleas, too proud to give you her
  reply.
The battle is not lost: keep your flag flying high!

Attend her all you can; for man who goes
  a-wooing
Must be polite, yet persevere in his pursuing:
Who knows what other swain's affections may
  be brewing?
A maiden's changing heart is many a man's
  undoing!

*The Art of Love*

And so you must take care to teach your lips the
   skill
Of amorous demand, bolder and bolder still,
To make the damsel's heart yearn for your love,
   until
You hold within your power her passion, mind
   and will.

Once you possess her love securely, I advise
That you seek worldly wealth: opulence
   beautifies
A gallant gentleman in any lady's eyes.
For when man's purse is full, maid's favor never
   dies.

And then, if you would rise still higher in her
   esteem,
Hang on her every word. Assure her that you
   deem
Her beauty unsurpassed. Tell her she reigns
   supreme,
Unrivaled sovereign of your every thought and
   dream.

If she has friends, you must dote on these damsels
   too:
Let your tongue pay its court to all her retinue.
Then one and all will say: "Blessed be the
   woman who
Nurtured this youth!" And they will praise and
   flatter you.

As for love's enemies—those slandering rogues of
   base
And infamous design, knaves of ignoble race—
To them as well you must present a friendly face,

Lest their deceitful tongues cover you with
   disgrace.

Greet all her household folk with courtesy.
   Befriend
Especially the girls—the single ones! Pretend
That you will bring them gifts galore: they will
   commend
Your kind and generous heart, and help you gain
   your end.

Take care that one and all esteem you courteous.
Then, if the maiden should, at times, hear men
   discuss
Your excellence, she will give ear with pride, and
   thus
Rejoice to be in love with one so virtuous.

Later, if you should be alone with her, request
A kiss—but tactfully—and if she should protest,
Then kiss her all the same, as if in idle jest.
Ladies who answer no, wish they had acquiesced.

The more her lips are kissed, the more your arms
   are twined
About her neck, the more will she yield heart
   and mind.
For kisses are the means—you will most surely
   find—
That man may best employ to master
   womankind.

Kiss her and hold her fast. Then, gently taking
   care
To do no hurt or harm, lay her down then and
   there;

With one hand lift her gown, then place the
    other square
Upon her sex, but with a playful, sportive air.

Now when she feels your hand, she may, indeed,
    demur.
She may cry out: "Off, off! I do not like you,
    sir!"
But let her shout and shriek her fill: you shall not
    stir.
Press your bare bodies close, and do your will
    with her.

Once you have snatched away the maiden's
    virgin treasure,
No more will she resist: you may proceed at
    leisure
To use her as you choose. Yet you must keep
    good measure;
For if you overdo, you will undo the pleasure.

And if her virtues find full favor in your sight;
If she is constant, true and faithful, then unite
Your lives at once. Do not hold wedlock in
    despite:
Mankind will honor you, and God will take
    delight.

But if, contrariwise, she treats you haughtily,
And if she lacks good sense, then keep your
    fancy free:
Renounce her and be off. Soon you will clearly
    see
How little was her love, how great her vanity.

Madmen who spurn their cure are fools indeed.
    However,

GUIART

Others there are who would find folly's cure, but
    never
Know where to look. And so, for them let me
    endeavor
To teach the remedies that banish love forever.

Take my advice: the cure is easy to achieve.
To learn how false the lady is, appear naïve,
Free of distrustful doubt, and easy to deceive.
But contemplate her face some night as you take
    leave.

Next morning, go again to see her, but before
She has the time to hide that face beneath her
    store
Of powders, plasters, paints, greases and gums
    galore.
Look at her only once, and you will love no
    more.

Or, if her beauty proves not to be counterfeit—
If she is fair and smooth of flesh, and exquisite
Of form—then turn your eyes away, lest you
    permit
Your folly to grow worse, instead of curing it.

Does she have ugly teeth, eyes that grow red and
    blear?
Then make her laugh and weep. Are you
    dismayed to hear
Her voice? Then make her sing—or bray!—
    long, loud and clear.
Her faults must ever be before your eye and ear.

Next you must learn to shun all those who live
    within

The lady's household: all her servants, friends
  and kin.
Then find some distant place where she has never
  been,
And, fleeing from her sight, go off and dwell
  therein.

But if one day, by chance, the lady happens by,
Then heed my counsel, friend: turn on your heel
  and fly
Before she sees you. For her heart will surely try
To capture for its own all that delights her eye.

If Jesus Christ our Lord has generously blessed
Her body's every part with all the comeliest
Of shape, then turn your thoughts far from her
  beauty, lest
It ever fill your mind, and leave your heart no
  rest.

Some morning, if she sends her messenger,
  become
Boorish and blunt: decry the endless tedium
Of lover's folly, grown woeful and wearisome.
Tell him that none but fools prolong their
  martyrdom.

And yet, try though you may, if you cannot
  abjure
The lady's love, and if you cannot long endure
To put her from your mind, then let me teach
  the cure
That every season brings to love's discomfiture.

In January's chill, when winter grips the year,
When earth is white, and air is wet, and sky is
  drear,

Go where your friends abound: good fellowship
   and cheer
Are quick to make man's woe and worry
   disappear.

And when the winter frost has passed, and
   everything
Seems to come back to life in the sweet breath of
   spring,
Go to the orchards; watch the tillers as they
   bring
Saplings to plant, in hope of handsome harvesting.

In summer's heat you can find much to occupy
Your days—long rows of wheat to hoe, young
   vines to tie—
Until the autumn, when your labors multiply,
And you reap bounty from the earth, and set it
   by.

But if all comes to naught—if you cannot subdue
Your passion—then, my friend, you should at
   once pursue
A second mistress. For the Scriptures tell us true:
One master must suffice, no man can toil for
   two.[12]

Likewise man cannot serve two ladies and sustain
Passion for both; new love will cause the old to
   wane.
Should this invention fail, the consequence is
   plain:
Leave home and land behind...no other cures
   remain.

And if you will not quit your kin, reflect a bit
Upon the sinful life. He who succumbs to it

Gains transient pleasure, but his loss is infinite:
Our Lord's and Lady's grace. So says the Holy
    Writ.

Behold this senseless world! Can men not realize
Its arrant falsity? How many jeopardize
Their soul's salvation, bent on faithless
    enterprise!
They know no truth, no trust; they live but lust
    and lies.

In the Almighty's name, my gentle lord, efface
From your desire and deed all that is mean and
    base.
Pay heed to me, if you would learn how to
    embrace
God's way, and earn the gift of His eternal grace.

For those who would know bliss, those who
    would be possessed
Of God, and dwell among His everlasting blessed,
Must spurn the evil works of the Unholiest,
And put aside all vain and earthly interest.

Baptism cleansed the guilt of mankind's origin
From your immortal soul; but if a life of sin
Has soiled your soul again, cast off your dark
    chagrin:
God pardons all whose prayer is pure and
    genuine.

Confession of one's sins, repenting earnestly,
And penance humbly done: these are, in truth,
    the three
Essential acts by which the sinful man may be
Restored to peace with God, in holy
    harmony. . . .

# On Courtesy

ANONYMOUS

THE ANGLO-NORMAN POEM *De courtoisie*—a
title conferred by its editor—is an early ver-
nacular specimen of a genre at least as old as
the Book of Proverbs: advice to a young man on
how to succeed in life. The Middle Ages had a great
hunger for collections of aphorisms, the ethical char-
acter of which has little or no Christian coloring. Al-
though *De courtoisie* belongs above all to this wis-
dom-literature, at the same time it is an etiquette
book: this is the author's promise in his opening lines,
where he offers lessons in "good sense" and "cour-
tesy." His precepts, set forth in octosyllabic coup-
lets to the length of 258 verses, follow no clearly
marked pattern. They propose a prudent, orderly,
bourgeois existence based on certain ethical prin-
ciples, but above all on the very practical one of
avoiding actions which may rebound on the doer:
do not make fun of others, others will make fun of
you; do not make threats in anger if you cannot
execute them; do not swear, for the more you swear,
the less you will be believed. The chief aim is to ac-
quire the esteem of the respectable in a rough, hard-
bitten society. To this end one should stick to the
old ways, the old friends, not speak too much, keep
secrets, keep out of taverns where fights and feuds
begin, listen politely without fidgeting when spoken
to. . . . So the list grows, more dreary, more banal,
with each passing couplet.

Embedded in the work are two passages of—in
the circumstances—surprising idealism: they speak
of love. These are the passages translated below
(verses 1–62; 114–39 and 150–55 of the original).

Curiously combining Christian and Ovidian elements with the attitudes of the courtly romances, they make an odd contrast with the pedestrian advice of the remainder of the poem. Notable is the praise of giving as a way to the lady's heart. Ovid advises it; but this is giving on a kingly scale: food and drink to all, horses to knights, jewels to ladies, church livings to clerics, husbands to widows. . . . No one is overlooked. But the note of self-interested prudence returns all too soon to becloud whatever grace love may have conferred.

*Text: De courtoisie* has been edited by E. Stengel, *Zeitschrift für franzosische Sprache und Literatur* 14 (1892), "Handschriftliches aus Oxford: Sec. 4. Ein Lehrgedicht in Reimpaaren: De courtoisie," 151–53.

### BIBLIOGRAPHICAL NOTE

There is no study other than Stengel's, which gives simply bibliographical data.

Good sir, if it should be your pleasure
To hear disclosed, in ample measure,
The precepts of gentility,
I pray that you give ear to me.
For if you listen as you ought,
You will be well and wisely taught.
First, you should take the greatest care
To cultivate a gentle air
And manner mild. You must, as well,
Avoid the playful damosel
Whose mind is ever folly-bent.
For, when she finds no devilment
In him who binds his heart to hers,
She neither dallies nor demurs,
But will, indeed—though some may doubt—
Promptly proceed to throw him out.
But if true love is your desire,
Good sir, let truth alone inspire
Your every thought: you must impress
The lady with your faithfulness,
And with a genuine display
Of frank and artless naïveté.
I do not say that you should spurn
A certain modest self-concern;
But never let it turn to pride
And arrogance unjustified.
The haughty man believes that he
Is God's gift to Humanity:
He thinks that even Roland could
Not boast of half his manlihood.
Yet though he deems his valor such,
He is not even worth as much
As Oliver! Then too, he will
Esteem himself more knightly still

ANONYMOUS

Than that most perfect cavalier
Of spotless soul and conscience clear,
Nephew of Arthur, Sir Gawain.
And such a man will be so vain
That he will think himself, in truth,
Fairer than Horn, that handsome youth,
Or even Prince Ipomedon,
Known as the very paragon
Of manly beauty, unsurpassed.[13]
Thus I beseech you, sir, to cast
Aside your self-conceit, and teach
Your pompous pride to underreach!
Next, you must try, in all you do,
To let discretion govern you:
Never rush off with headlong speed
Into a rash and reckless deed.
But, rather, weigh the consequence
And issue of your actions; whence
It follows clearly that you should
Choose only those that lead to good,
Refusing all that lead to ill.
Obey this counsel and you will
Ever appear in mankind's eyes
Worthy and just and worldly-wise.
Love God, as Christians must, above
All else; and since we speak of love,
Never neglect to love your neighbor:
When harsh his lot and hard his labor,
Offer him all the help you can.
Thus should you serve both God and man.
For loving homage, duly done,
Brings myriad blessings one by one—
Above all, that which man may render
To creatures of the female gender:
God looks with favor, you will find,
On worship paid to womankind!
For women are the very source

Of fame, wealth, valor, joy—perforce,
Of all the best there is; and hence,
I fear that he has lost his sense
Who, by his actions, seems to be
Glad to incur their enmity.
Though he may strive and strain forever,
Fortune will frown on his endeavor. . . .

And so, I hope and trust, good sir,
That true and proper love may stir
Your heart with its ennobling passion.
For when you love in worthy fashion,
The more, in truth, will you discover
What best behooves the gallant lover:
Pure in intent, you will select
A conduct courtly and correct;
And you will wisely leave behind
All deeds uncouth and unrefined.
Here let a word or two suffice
To give some sage and sound advice:
Whenever woman acquiesces,
Never go vaunting your successes;
Else you will lose, beyond recall,
Your porridge—platter, pot and all!
And you will be despised, decried,
Disdained by ladies far and wide.
And now, a rule which you had best
Firmly implant within your breast:
Learn how to give with generous hand.
Let one and all, throughout the land,
Enjoy the bounty of your table;
As for the champions of your stable,
Bestow them with a gracious air
On valiant knights and debonair.
To ladies you shall give such things
As silken sashes, clasps and rings;
While to the lovely damosels,

Baubles and blooms and bagatelles. . . .
But do take care, for Heaven's sake,
Lest, like so many men, you make
Promises that you know you will
Full well declare, yet not fulfill.
For such behavior lets the fool
Happily heap his ridicule,
Content that he can criticize
And lessen you in lady's eyes.
In short, no man should play the giver
Who is not sure he will deliver! . . .

ANONYMOUS

# Advice to Ladies

### ROBERT DE BLOIS

Robert de blois, the author of this *Advice to Ladies*, flourished in the second third of the thirteenth century. His surviving output of eleven thousand verses would indicate a professional: Robert left two romances, lyric verse, and didactic poems addressed to princes and ladies alike. The more than seven hundred and fifty lines of the *Advice* are thus but a small part of his total *œuvre*. They are intended for married ladies, one would imagine—for Robert does not specify his audience —of the *haute bourgeoisie*.

If the passages offered here in translation seem to lack continuity, it is because Robert de Blois's poem itself is but an unconnected series of precepts. It skips alarmingly from advice on behavior when returning from church (not translated here), to counsel on when to sing and when not, to hints on care of the hands, and so on. With perhaps unconscious cynicism, Robert de Blois seems at first sight to be calling attention to those areas of their lives where the ladies, in his observation, are most often at fault, and most in need of correction. It is in their dealings with others that he is interested—their conversation, their appearance, their conduct at table— and above all in their churchgoing, around which their days revolve. Their inner, spiritual life is of no concern to him. Yet even in his desire to help his readers become socially acceptable—and even more, be attractive to men, and know how to deal with their suitors—there is a strong underlying moral intention, which lends force to his precepts and sharpens his caustic aphorisms. Though he echoes

*Advice to Ladies*

many of the matters of the Ovidian tradition, he counters it, too, displaying some of the indignation of the preacher in his condemnation of foolish women, and expressing himself with the directness of speech of contemporary clerical satirists. There is no mincing of words over those who show too much of their fair flesh ("C'est signes de putaige," i.e., a sign of harlotry), or allow themselves to be kissed on the mouth, or fall into gluttonous, drunken habits. A well-turned line or couplet leaves no doubt of the poet's contempt of such creatures.

It is his wish to guide married ladies among these rocks and shoals of life, to show them the need for *mesure*, the golden mean, the middle way between excessive talking, for example, which enrages the bystander, and excessive silence, which encourages enterprising suitors to believe they have conquered. The lady lives surrounded by the malicious, ever alert to criticize her least failing, and eager to bestow on her an irretrievably bad reputation. It requires all Robert de Blois's advice to save her from an even worse menace: she is a prey to men, brutal opportunists watching for the slightest sign of favor, voluntary or involuntary, meaningful or not. One is reminded of Madame de Chartres's solemn warnings to the future Princesse de Clèves, in Madame de La Fayette's novel, to exercise the utmost prudence lest she be caught up in the prevailing *galanterie* of the court.

*Advice to Ladies* is flawed as a moral treatise by its author's latent antifeminism and by his ambivalent attitude. These ladies must be faithful to their marriage vows, he says with force, yet he has succeeded in composing an art of coquetry. The last two hundred lines of the poem constitute a delightful parody of the courtly love sung of by the lyric poets. A woman must know how to cope with such elegant tactics on the part of a would-be seducer, because she is bound to her husband. And then again she might someday wish to yield to her suitor.

64                    ROBERT DE BLOIS

There is nothing vaporously noble about love in Robert de Blois's opinion. It is one of the compelling drives of the flesh, and his concluding lines have all of Ovid's cynicism: Resist his advances if you will; if he loves you truly, he will love you all the more.

The subjects taken up by Robert de Blois, and the explicit, down-to-earth language he uses, have led some to believe that his intentions were more parodic than serious. It has been hard for French historians to accept so crude and vulgar a picture of thirteenth-century society, a society which a century of Courts of Love, of courtly poets and romancers is supposed to have refined and civilized. We cannot, of course, be sure of the author's intentions, after a lapse of seven hundred years, and his own ambivalences do not make a judgment easier. In general, *Advice to Ladies* accords with other manuals of the age in its precepts and with the satirists of society life in its general tone. And it must be said that compared with some of the tales of the *fabliaux*, it is restrained and polite. This worldly, pragmatic, unphilosophical, unidealistic collection of maxims of conduct would indeed seem to have been seriously intended, despite numerous ironies and levities of style.

Translated here are some five hundred of the original's seven hundred and fifty-seven lines, viz: 1–58, 97–111, 121–32, 145–68, 169–88, 189–212, 213–38, 255–68, 301–16, 343–72, 373–92, 393–414, 453–62, 469–76, 497–511, 521–28, 539–54, 565–648, 649–83, 684–757.

*Text:* John Howard Fox, *Robert de Blois, son œuvre didactique et narrative* (Paris, 1950), pp. 133–55.

BIBLIOGRAPHICAL NOTE

The principal studies are: Charles-Victor Langlois, *La Vie en France au moyen âge de la fin du douzième au milieu du quatorzième siècle d'après des moralistes du temps* (Paris, 1925); Alice A. Hentsch, *De la littérature didactique du moyen âge s'adressant spécialement aux femmes* (Cahors, 1903); Edmond Faral, *La Vie quotidienne au temps de Saint Louis* (Paris, 1942). The account in Thomas F. Crane, *Italian Social Customs of the Sixteenth Century* (New Haven, 1920), pp. 344–46, places the *Chastoiement* in a general context, but destroys its particular flavor.

Ladies will pay but little mind
To this, my book, unless they find
Their manners much improved thereby.
So listen, one and all, while I
Offer you lessons, which, if learned,
Will grace you with the love, well earned,
Of God and man; for courteous ways
Win both divine and human praise.
Therefore I wish, with all due tact,
To teach our ladies how to act:
How they should go, how they should come,
When best to speak, and when keep mum.
Let them avoid extremes, and thus
Be neither mute nor garrulous.
For it is said that babbling creatures
Have studied with unseemly teachers.
And she of whom it may be stated:
"She talks too much," will be berated
Round and about for foolishness.
Therefore a lady should express
Herself in measured manner, lest
She be the butt of jeer and jest.
Withal, it is no less unwise
To be too silent: men misprize
Ladies who show no inclination
To hold a decent conversation.
Woman cannot be certain, therefore,
What kind of conduct man will care for.
If she displays a courteous bent,
With words of gentle grace, well meant,
To one and all who come her way—
Be they mere squire or *chevalier*—
And if she tenders each his due,
Too often they will misconstrue

Her courtliness, and each will boast
That she, in truth, loves him the most
(Though none of these gay cavaliers
Could win her in a hundred years!).
If, on the other hand, she greets
With mild reserve the men she meets,
They will be quick to seek the meaning,
Calling her proud, prim, overweening,
Mindless or mad, imputing to her
Scurrilous traits that could undo her.
Thus many a lady coldly turns
Away from Love's delights, and spurns
Those men who—were she not afraid—
Might see their efforts well repaid.
In short, the woman wooed must use
Much moderation, lest she lose
The good esteem that she possesses.
For man makes fun of both excesses;
And many a high repute can fall
From "too much" or from "none at all." . . .


### ADVICE REGARDING THE BOSOM

Take care not to allow your breast
To be felt, fondled or caressed
By any hands save those that ought.
For, true it is, when one first thought
Of fashioning the clothing clasp,
It was to keep man's lustful grasp
From woman's bust, which should be known
To husband's hands and his alone.
(For husbands may touch what they choose,
Since, for their pleasure, they may use
Their ladies as they wish; and wives
Must lead submissive, duteous lives,
Obedient as the monk or friar,
Who bends the knee before his prior.)


68                              ROBERT DE BLOIS

And so, one made the tunic pin
To keep hands out and bosoms in. . . .


### ADVICE REGARDING THE MOUTH

Next I would warn you, ladies, lest
You let man's lips to yours be pressed—
Save only his, to whom you owe
Your all. For, as you surely know,
When lady's lips are freely kissed,
The rest of her cannot resist:
A kiss can lead to so much more!
Soon she begins to hunger for
Kiss after kiss; and then she will
Not cease her sport, indeed, until
She finds some place in which she may
Proceed to give the rest away. . . .


### ADVICE REGARDING THE GLANCE

Unless you love a man with true
And proper love, beware lest you
Frequently look his way. Be wise,
And take care where you turn your eyes:
Unseemly habits, left unchecked,
Bring only blame and disrespect.
For man, when he takes cognizance
Of lady's oft-repeated glance,
Will misconstrue and be inclined
To think that she has love in mind.
Nor is it strange that he should make
Such an unfortunate mistake:
Often I find that, to my woe,
Where heart is, there the eyes will go.
The glance is lovers' go-between;
If lady's glances do not mean
What man believes, then surely she

ROBERT DE BLOIS

Deceives him most capriciously.
But since a lady's heart is vain,
Her eyes will never long remain
At rest; like hawk about to snare
A lark, she casts them everywhere.
Thus many ladies compromise
Their reputations with their eyes.

### CONCERNING BOASTFULNESS

If man makes amorous overture,
I urge you, ladies, to be sure
Not to go flaunting your success,
Gloating with braggart boorishness.
Be modest when he dotes on you
With one intent: to wit, to woo.
For if, at length, you should decide
To do his will, how could you hide
Your tender liaison from those
Who heard you boast? One never knows
When, in an instant, love may find
The chance to change one's heart and mind:
Many a haughty lass has learned
That would-be lover, loudly spurned,
Can yet become the heart's delight
Of one who never dreamed he might.
Tomorrow you may well give way
To him whose suit you scorn today.
In short, if man would be your lover,
Take care to keep it under cover.

### CONCERNING THE EXPOSURE
### OF THE FLESH

A lady errs, in truth, if she
Displays her flesh immodestly
In any but her husband's sight.

*Advice to Ladies*

Some, who would show how fair and white
Their breasts, go almost bosom-bare,
For one and all; while some take care
To leave the side exposed, and show
Some flesh above, some flesh below.
Still others think that thigh and knee
Are there for all the world to see,
And show, beneath a hem held high,
More than is meant to meet the eye.
The gentleman will not admire
Such lustful ways, for base desire
Brings only pain; and wise men say:
"Eyes are the source of heart's dismay."
White neck and throat, white hands and face—
These parts give promise of the grace
That lies beneath the gown, concealed;
And they may freely be revealed
Without reproof. But, be it known,
They are the most that may be shown.
She who delights in bold undress
Commits an act of wickedness
And folly, which we all deplore,
For it befits none but the whore.


### ADVICE REGARDING THE REFUSAL OF GIFTS

Beware of men who make too free
With gifts of costly finery;
Ladies who crave such gifts soon learn
What they must offer in return!
But she who holds her honor high
Will shun those men who try to buy
A lady's love with jewel and gem,
And she will have no part of them:
Gifts such as these will cost far more
Than ever she had bargained for.
How many a lady's soul lies lost

ROBERT DE BLOIS

Because she paid despite the cost!
Greed is the power, alas, that makes
A wench commit such dire mistakes,
Grievous to God and humankind.
For she who takes must bear in mind
That she will also give: in sum
Her virtue must, in time, succumb
To deeds that cannot but disparage—
Indeed, destroy—a worthy marriage.
And so I say, rich though it be,
No jewel is worth your chastity. . . .

### ADMONITION REGARDING QUARRELSOME TEMPER

Above all else, I must denounce
Those ladies ever quick to pounce
And carp in quarrelsome dissent.
You may be sure that men resent
These crabbed creatures, for they say:
"Alas, no lovely lasses they!"
Indeed, one would do well to call
Such would-be ladies strumpets all.
For bickering ends in bitterness;
And though a lady may possess
Beauty and charm, yet men are blind
To her attractions once they find
That she delights in wildly wagging
A tongue that never tires of nagging!
And so it seems that ladies, truly,
Must be unstrung, who carp unduly. . . .

### ADMONITION REGARDING GLUTTONY

Next, let a warning word suffice
If you would shun the foulest vice
To which a lady may submit,

*Advice to Ladies*

Most vulgar of them all: to wit,
The wicked sin of drunkenness
And gluttony. For one excess
Leads to another, graver still;
And she who gluts more than her fill
Of food and wine, soon finds a taste
For bold excess below the waist!
No worthy man will pay his court
To lady of such lowly sort,
Who revels in her drunken pleasure,
Toping and tippling past all measure!
For she who drinks more than she should,
Forfeits the charms of ladyhood:
Gone is her courtly, comely air,
Gone is her grace, her *savoir-faire*. . . .


### ADVICE REGARDING THE GREETING OF MEN
### AND THE LIFTING OF ONE'S VEIL

Ladies are thought unmannerly
If, when a man of high degree
Offers them greeting, they disdain
His salutation, and remain
Silent and veiled. In their defense
One may explain that reticence,
And not ill breeding, is to blame.
Yet man will wonder, all the same,
If she who shuts and masks her mouth
Has ugly teeth, foul breath, or both.
I see no harm if homely creatures
Keep themselves veiled to hide their features:
Ladies must not be criticized
Because they want their faults disguised.
But neither do I count as clever
Those who, though pretty, seem forever
Covered and cloaked, all veil-bedecked.
To them I pay no high respect;

For comeliness is, by repute,
Lady's most pleasing attribute.
Let those with faces pale and gaunt
Hang veils about them all they want.
But let no needless shrouds enclose
Well-favored teeth, lips, eyes and nose.
Exceptions will arise, of course:
To wit, when riding on your horse
Along the open thoroughfare,
You should not let your face stand bare.
Then too, when off to church, you will
Do well to keep it veiled until
You pass within the vestibule.
And if you fear the ridicule
Of those whose high regard you prize,
Because your smile offends the eyes,
Then, when you feel a laugh beginning,
Let hand be quick to hide your grinning.

### ADVICE REGARDING THE CONCEALMENT
### OF PALE COLOR AND FOUL ODOR

Now let me give advice to those
Whose ills repel man's eyes and nose:
Ladies whose cheeks are pale as death,
Or who, when they exhale their breath,
Cause everyone to wince, retreating.[14]
The cure for both lies in their eating:
The pallid ones should start each day
With ample food and drink, if they
Would learn how morning wine can bring
A glow to lady's coloring.
For you who smell, some kind of spice—
Anise or fennel—may suffice.
You must be sure, in any case,
Never to puff in someone's face.
(At mass, when you exchange the "kiss

Of peace," [15] pay special heed to this!)
Then too, you should take care to let
No man embrace you when you sweat.
For surely you must know full well,
The more you sweat, the more you smell.

## CONCERNING PROPER BEHAVIOR IN CHURCH

If you would act as ladies ought,
Here is a warning worth some thought,
One that you should not take in vain
Or treat with cynical disdain:
In church it is especially grave
If ladies choose to misbehave;
For many a prying eye will stare
To spy their every action there.
Nor do such pious, churchly eyes
Forget what once they recognize.
Too many a lass has curious notions
How to behave while at devotions:
Some will neglect to bend the knee
In earnest prayer; some seem to be
Forever bent on idle chatter
Or given to constant titter-tatter.
Others do not seek God, I fear,
But come to find a cavalier;
They cast their glances round about—
To right, to left, inside and out—
Forgetting that an eye too free
Betrays the heart's inconstancy.
In short, beware lest you besmirch
Your reputation while in church. . . .

## CONCERNING THE PROPER USE OF SINGING

If you can sing in accents clear,
With pleasing voice to charm the ear,
Sing out! At proper time and place

ROBERT DE BLOIS

Sweet song enhances comely grace.
But keep in mind, a lady should
Not sing too much, unless she would
Incur disfavor and displeasure:
To everything there is a measure.
So lest your music vex and bore,
Sing just enough and then no more. . . .

### CONCERNING THE CLEANLINESS OF THE HANDS

Your hands must be kept neat and clean,
With nails cut short, so that between
The flesh and nail no dirt may find
A place to thrive; for womankind
Must keep in mind that sweet success
May well depend on cleanliness:
Neatness and grace earn more respect
Than beauty dying of neglect. . . .

### ADVICE REGARDING BEHAVIOR AT MEALS

Be certain, also, when you eat,
To be especially discreet.
For men esteem those ladies who
Show that they know what not to do
When dining in their midst; while they
Who make indecorous display—
Crass and ill bred—will, bye the bye,
Be looked upon with scornful eye.
Thus, as you chew your food, be sure
Not to behave like brutish boor,
Talking and laughing, opening wide
Your mouth for all to see inside.
Is there a roast? Take my advice:
Never seek out the finest slice,
But always let another guest
Select the biggest and the best. . . .
Also, before a lady sips

*Advice to Ladies*

Her wine, she ought to wipe her lips;
For he who takes the flagon next
Is certain to be sorely vexed
By wine that has a fatty taste.
Nor should you be like those ill-graced,
Grease-fingered creatures who suppose
That they may wipe their eyes and nose
On table linen if they please.
Men scorn such gross vulgarities! . . .

### PROHIBITION AGAINST LYING

Here is another vice which you,
As well-bred ladies, must eschew:
The grievous sin of telling lies.
No gentleman will utter sighs
Of lovesick servitude for any
Lady whose lies are mean and many.
For man of worth and courtly station
Decries deceit and fabrication.
He would as soon be mauled and maimed
By sword or spear, as be proclaimed
A lying rogue. And rightly so;
For there is little here below
More vile in eyes of God and men
Than those who, time and time again,
Delight in fraud and counterfeit.
A wound may heal, a bone may knit,
The body's health may be restored:
But those who lie before the Lord
And fellow men, yet feel no shame,
Lose God's esteem and man's acclaim. . . .

### CONCERNING THOSE LADIES WHO DO NOT KNOW
### HOW TO TURN ASIDE AN AMOROUS SUITOR

Ladies are often caught up short
When men begin to pay them court.

Thus many a lady, to her woe,
Has never learned to answer no;
But there she stands, naïvely mute,
While would-be lover, pressing suit,
Misjudges her bewilderment
And, taking silence for consent,
Rejoices in a victory
Easily won. And yet, if he
Lays hands on what he claims as his,
He soon finds out how wrong he is!
And so, to serve your honor best,
Learn to refuse what men request.
Indeed, even when ladies choose
To give their love, let them refuse
Man's first advances, and make clear
That, even though he persevere,
Never can he be sure to win.
For love that comes without chagrin
Brings far less pleasure in its train
Than love that comes with toil and pain:
The worse the ills we must endure,
So all the sweeter is the cure;
And sunshine never seems more fair
Than after rain has filled the air.
Consider, too, what men must think
Of ladies who, quick as a wink,
Yield heart and body: one, two, three!
"If she will play so fast and free
With me, then surely I can guess
How promptly she must answer 'yes'—
Without a 'who?' or 'what?' or 'why?'—
To any man who winks an eye,
Or nonchalantly nods his head
With beckoning glances toward the bed."
Thus, whether you would grant or spurn
A man's entreaties, you must learn—
For all those reasons named above—
How to say "no" when he says "love."

*Advice to Ladies*

And so, give ear while I explain
How to rebuff the amorous swain
Who will appear—from who knows where?—
And, feigning deep and dark despair,
Complain that life has fast become
A woeful, weary martyrdom
Without your love; and who will say:
"Mercy, Milady! Night and day,
I cannot sleep, nor eat, nor drink;
But languish, and grow pale, and sink
Deeper into my hopeless plight."
And on and on he will recite,
With ample store of "oh" and "ah,"
"Alas," "alack," *et cetera*...
Until, at length, he will profess
That you, and you alone, possess
The power to free him from a fell
And deadly fate: "Fair damosel,
You are my life, my death, my joy,
My agony; you can destroy
Or make me well. And so I plead,
For love of God, that you will heed
My last appeal for clemency:
Mercy, Milady! Pity me,
Your loyal-hearted swain, who prays
That God above may find the ways
And means to make you mine! Ah, bliss!
I seek no fairer fate than this!"
At which point, if his voice is strong,
He may burst forth in plaintive song,
Hoping that you cannot refuse
To be seduced by lyric muse:

THE LOVER'S COMPLAINT

"Milady, source of my distress,
Through days and nights of bitterest pain,

I sigh for your hardheartedness
And only cease to sigh again.
My life is yours: let not the bane
Of love condemn me, comfortless,
To languish in your cruel disdain.

I gaze with pleasure and delight
On flawless face and body fair,
That whet my eager appetite
Then force my passion to forbear.
Such is my hapless heart's despair;
And though I may my eyes indict,
Yet all my being the woe must share.

The joyous birds flit to and fro
In twittering homage to the spring.
Like them I sing my song; but oh!
'Tis but to hide my sorrowing.
Fair face, fair heart, fair everything!
For you, I fear, death lays me low,
Unless you soothe my suffering.

Yet though I ache and agonize,
I shall not clamor or protest.
Let me but feast my eager eyes
At will, upon that comeliest
Of form and feature, beauty-blessed.
Then shall I cease my soulful sighs
And know the cure for my unrest.

Do with me what you choose to do;
Treat me like chattel, if you will.
Your loyal liege, I do not rue
Love's pain, but bear it staunch and still:
Yours to ordain, mine to fulfill.
Cursed be the faithless lover who
Repents the love that does him ill."

When you have heard his dire lament,
Then tell him this: "Sire, my intent
Is not to do you injury.
Thus, if you pout and pine for me,
And suffer all the pain you say,
Your heart, I fear, leads you astray.
I should prefer to see you, Sire,
Hearty and hale as you desire;
And so I do, indeed, regret
The woes that you bemoan. And yet,
I cannot love you—save as I
Love all good folk—and this is why:
Never shall I break faith, please Heaven,
With him to whom my troth is given.
I love but one alone, no more;
For, by the Holy Church, I swore
Love, body and strict obedience
To none but him forever hence.
And thus my love, by God ordained,
Shall flourish pure and unprofaned.
One man alone knows my caress:
May Hell's dark force be powerless
To make a traitorous jade of me
And turn his love to enmity!
If I betray him, I shall earn
Only his loathing in return.
His worth is such that, truth to tell,
I cannot love him half so well
As he deserves; thus I endeavor
Humbly to do his will, whatever
His pleasure may demand of me.
Now Sire, in all sincerity,
Tell me what virtue you can find
In creature of my lowly kind!

Do you think me a simple soul,
Easy to cozen and cajole
With honeyed words? Come now, good Sire!
My loveliness does not inspire
Man's mind to madness! And, indeed,
Were I of such a beauteous breed
As you suggest, I should take care
Lest any man might find me fair;
I should detest that comely face
That could but lead to my disgrace.
I pray to God that I remain
Honest and true, though I be plain;
And that He ever keep me free
Of beauty-born iniquity.
You call me fair; and yet I know,
In truth, you do not find me so,
But wish to mock my common sense,
And jibe and jest at my expense.
I am distressed that you would deem
Me worthy of such a low esteem
That I should serve your waggish wit.
But let us speak no more of it,
Good Sire! I have already heard
Too many a false, disheartening word.
Pray hold your tongue, or I shall flee
From every place you chance to be;
And, by the saints, your insolence
Will bring my friends to my defense."
Be careful while you thus orate,
Lest laughter mar your stern, sedate
And somber statements of reproof.
Yet neither should you stay aloof,
Speaking your piece in haughty guise
With accents that may jeopardize
The high regard in which you stand.
Chide him with measured reprimand,
Neither too mild nor too severe.

*Advice to Ladies*

83

Behaving thus, you will endear
Yourself still more, and he will praise
Your courteous air and winsome ways.
Then, bye the bye, you will discover
That if you want him for your lover,
And if you give him cause enough,
He will forget your long rebuff,
And, like all lovesick gentlemen,
Come falling at your feet again.
While some there are who feign love's woe,
Yet there is many a faithful beau
Who, though distraught by pain and anguish,
All the more loyal seems to languish,
True to the love that he has chosen...
"When hard the freeze, the more lies frozen!" [16]

ROBERT DE BLOIS

# "On the Rules of Love" from
# The Book of Love

DROUART LA VACHE

ABOUT THE YEAR 1185, ANDREAS CAPELLANUS COM-
posed a book which was to know consider-
able celebrity: *De amore libri tres,* sometimes
called *De arte honeste amandi* (a title generally
translated as *On the Art of Courtly Love,* even
though the word "courtly" is question-begging, and
perhaps simply incorrect). A hundred years later, it
was well known. Jean de Meun used its definition
of love in his part of the *Romance of the Rose,* and
in 1277 the bishop of Paris included it in a list of
prohibited works and propositions. The bishop not-
withstanding, vernacular translations began to ap-
pear: Énanchet turned it into Franco-Italian prose
in 1285; in 1290, Drouart la Vache reworked it in
French verse; a Tuscan translation had already ap-
peared, and another was done in the fourteenth
century; and a Catalan translation was made in the
same century. Andreas's work has been available for
some time in English in John Jay Parry's translation.
Offered here is a translation of Drouart la Vache's
version of the "Rules of Love."

Drouart chose standard octosyllabic couplets,
varying the length of his rules from two to six lines.
This form, the differing linguistic possibilities of
Latin and Old French, and Drouart's own gifts,
make a distinct contrast with Andreas's prose. Latin
seems to have been created expressly for concise
maxims and lapidary inscriptions. Drouart prefers
the concrete to the abstract, giving his translation

*"On the Rules of Love"*

a less imperious ring, and a more immediate, more human tone. True, necessities of rhyme lead here and there to excess wordage, and yet may serve to clarify Andreas's compactness. The dry sound of Andreas's rule 1 carries compelling legal force: "Causa coniugii ab amore non est excusatio recta," i.e., marriage is no lawful excuse from loving. Drouart's translation brings us back to the world of men and women. One would conclude that the Latin rules, being expressed so precisely and authoritatively, must have carried more weight, and that the clerics were right, in their age-old debate with knights, in maintaining that they were superior lovers. For the knights, after all, were using a far less exacting set of rules than their rivals.

Although he sometimes adds nuances not in the original, Drouart follows his source quite faithfully for the most part. He does, however, seem to misunderstand Andreas's rule 12, which requires the true lover to desire only his beloved's embraces (rather than, as Drouart has it, to avoid embraces taken by force). As for the order in which the rules are given, Drouart's is not altogether that of his model: he translates in the order 1, 4, 2, 3, 5, 6, 7, 8, 9, 10, 11, 12, 13, 14, 15, 16, 17, 18, 19, 23, 20, 21, 24 and 25 (Drouart's 23), 26, 27, 28, 29, 30, 31. As the preceding indicates, he combines two of the rules (24, 25), and omits one (22), thus reducing Andreas's total of 31 to 29.

*Text:* R. Bossuat, ed., *Li Livres d'amours de Drouart la Vache* (Paris, 1926), verses 6485–6572.

BIBLIOGRAPHICAL NOTE

John Jay Parry, trans. and ed., *The Art of Courtly Love by Andreas Capellanus*, Records of Civilization, no. 33 (New York, 1941).
There is no study of Drouart in English. The true significance of Andreas's work is the object of much

controversy. See, for example, D. W. Robertson, Jr., *A Preface to Chaucer* (Princeton, 1962), and Peter Dronke's review of Felix Schlösser, *Andreas Capellanus: Seine Minnelehre und das Christliche Weltbild um 1200* (Bonn, 1960), in *Medium Ævum* 32, no. 1 (1963).

I come now to the rules of Love,
Eager, at last, to speak thereof.

The first declares that wedlock's laws
Never give woman proper cause
For saying no, and coldly thwarting
The gallant suitor come a-courting.[17]

The second rule, in turn, makes plain
That Love must always wax or wane:
One or the other—so it goes.

As for the third, it clearly shows
That no lad truly loves unless
He fears his lady's faithlessness.

Next, be advised: two loves together
Cannot, at once, hold man in tether.

Nor shall man's pleasure find fulfilling
In kisses snatched from lips unwilling,
Or in the cold caress, ill got,
Of lass who loves him not a jot.

The sixth rule tells us this: a youth
Must be of proper years, in truth,
Before he may be loved;[18] to wit,
The marriage age is requisite.

Should lady's lover chance to die,
First she must let two years go by—
No more, no less. When this is done,
Let her go find a second one.[19]

Layman or clerk, no man should be
Bereft of lady needlessly.

Never, indeed, can Love abide
With sinful Avarice, side by side.

Next, man must learn it best behooves him
Only to woo when true love moves him.

As for the miss, he must not choose her
If as a wife he would refuse her.

The loyal lover must not try
To force his lass to satisfy
His lustful wish against her will.[20]

Learn too, Love only lasts until
That moment when it stands revealed:
To live, Love must remain concealed.

Ladies who lightly acquiesce
Before a lover's eagerness,
And quickly grant his wish, will find
That man is usually inclined
To prize them less, so soon acceding,
Than those he wins by prayer and pleading.

When loved one speaks or comes in view,[21]
Lovers must turn a pallid hue.

And when they suddenly behold
Their lass, they tremble uncontrolled.[22]

Then too, a new love, bye and bye,
Must make the old take leave and fly.

Worthy to love is man who leads
An upright life of virtuous deeds.

Love, when it once grows weak and sickly,
Proceeds to perish all too quickly:

Do what it will, Love on the wane
Never will know good health again.

The love-tormented suitor barely
Can eat or drink, and sleeps but rarely.

He who gives Love his whole attention
Always knows fear and apprehension.

Jealousy makes Love's yearning grow,
Along with all its pain and woe.

The man who woos with all his love
Surely puts no desire above
The wish that every thought and action
Be to his lady's satisfaction.

No loyal swain can fail to do
All that his loved one wants him to.

The joy of Love's caress is such,
No suitor ever can get too much.

Even the slightest supposition
Quickly provokes a lad's suspicion
Against his lass—though, just for this,
One would not say he hates the miss.[23]

No one can fancy loving truly
Who lusts for fleshly joys unduly.

The loyal lover, ever musing
Upon the lady of his choosing,
Finds no relief: look here, look there—
He seems to see her everywhere.

There is no edict, no decree,
That says one woman may not be

EVERYWHERE

"On the Rules of Love"

Openly loved by suitors twain.
In like regard, a single swain
May find himself—in blameless fashion—
The object of two ladies' passion.

# Advice on Love

RICHARD DE FOURNIVAL

T HE SIMPLE TITLE, *Advice on Love*, PROMISES
less than this prose treatise has to offer. The
work surveys human love in all its manifold
aspects, distinguishing, defining, and classifying in
characteristic medieval style. At the root of all lies
romantic love, subject of the author's warm praise
and advocacy, and subject of the advice that he is
eager to give. The author, Richard de Fournival
(1201–60), was in his day a well-connected, influ-
ential personage. Son of Roger de Fournival, physi-
cian to the king of France, he was a physician him-
self, before becoming a deacon and later chancellor
of the cathedral of Amiens during the episcopate of
his half-brother, Arnoul (1236–47). As an ecclesias-
tic, he was obliged to seek permission to continue
to perform minor surgery. As chancellor, he admin-
istered the affairs of the diocese, defended its rights,
and on occasion intervened on behalf of citizens of
Amiens as far afield as Westminster. Nor did he fail
to defend the perquisites of his own office against
his brother's successor to the see.

Richard's literary remains bear witness to his
versatility. He has been a strong candidate for au-
thorship of an anonymous Latin poem, 2,400 hex-
ameters long, the pseudo-Ovidian *De vetula*, known
in translation as *The Old Woman or Ovid's Last
Love*. He composed in Latin an unusual biblio-
graphical work, *Biblionomia*, which catalogues the
contents of a public library in Amiens (1243), per-
haps the first public library in the Middle Ages,
possibly founded by Richard himself. It contained a
wide range of books, and the extensive list of medi-

*Advice on Love*

93

cal works that Richard compiled is accompanied by his own professional remarks. Musically gifted, he composed a score of chansons, with verse in Picard French. His *Bestiary of Love* reveals the secular bent of a well-educated mind. The bestiaries, repositories of the zoological lore of the age, attribute edifying symbolic meanings to beasts, birds, and fishes; Richard de Fournival sees them in a worldly, erotic light. Love, indeed, preoccupies him. In addition to the *Bestiary* and the *Advice,* he composed a third prose work in French, the *Power of Love.* All his interests are in some degree reflected in the *Advice on Love,* here translated.

The title of the work recalls the insatiable medieval thirst for advice from father (presumably experienced) to inexperienced offspring. *On Courtesy* is such a poem, *Advice to Ladies* is similar. Richard de Fournival is afflicted with the same malady, a desire to inflict his opinions on his hearer in solemn tones of admonition, even though he claims more than once that experience is the only true teacher in matters of love. Although he has read Andreas Capellanus's *On the Art of Courtly Love,* he avoids the ironic, cautionary tone of Andreas's address to his probably fictional Walter, and expresses delight in responding to the request of his own probably equally fictional sister.

The treatise is striking in the clarity of its organization and the breadth of its information. It falls essentially into two parts, after prefatory remarks: a general survey of love in all its ramifications, and an analysis and advocacy of a particular kind, romantic love. An epilogue claims to relate a personal experience of the author's, which convinced him that he too must pursue the love of which he speaks. The general survey displays an easy, confident, almost professorial grasp of the tradition that ultimately goes back to Cicero and to Aristotle. Richard is thoroughly conversant with the twelfth-century Christianizers of Cicero, Aelred of Rievaulx and

Pierre de Blois, who, in turn, followed the patristic tradition that reinforced Cicero's teachings with scriptural example and quotation, and converted the dialogue *On Friendship* to Christian purposes. It is more than likely that Richard's deft general survey of love, which retains this peculiar blend of biblical and Ciceronian quotation—strange to modern ideas yet hallowed in his day—owes everything to current school formulations of the nature of love and friendship. Hence his garbled quotations of Cicero and even of Ovid, from whom he takes words but no substance.

Richard knows that love in general may be either good or evil. Good love may be either spiritual or temporal. Spiritual may be defined in terms of Cicero's famous definition of friendship allied to the words of the two Great Commandments; temporal may be the instinctive love of parents for their off-spring, of family, or it may simply be heartfelt love. Such heartfelt affection may be either a general love of humanity or a particular, deep-rooted love for one person alone. Richard has thus led us skillfully down the branches of the genealogical tree of love, to the one love that truly interests him here, the heartfelt love for one person alone. Though in the medieval treatises, this particular friend, the *amicus specialis*, is traditionally another man, another Pylades to an Orestes, Richard's *Advice* is concerned with defining and advocating this unique relationship between man and woman. Here lies the interest of his work, and Richard goes about developing his subject with characteristic precision.

Richard had perceived with an unsentimental eye that his sister was ready to engage in love by reason of her age and appropriate physical development. Now he exhorts her: "Time and Nature beckon," the Scriptures, our Lord himself approve of young love. Systematically he proceeds from definition and description of love to state the moment of its conception, the quality of the hearts involved, the manner and place of its conception, its three stages (inception, assertion, confirmation), and the three maladies of love, then concludes with advice on coping with accidental or deliberate delays in love's progress. Andreas Capellanus helped him here. Though Richard claims to have learned a great deal himself, he must confess that he can teach but a fraction of what personal experience alone can impart. An epilogue tells of a frightening youthful experience that compelled him to accept love's commands. Alas for his adventures: this callow knight was called into being by Andreas's pages, too.

What the end of this love might be, Richard does not make clear. It certainly is not the animal love of compulsive seducers, which is evil and to be shunned. The young lady must not forget the love of God; yet marriage is excluded on the grounds that a wife's love for her husband is an obligation, a duty. Heloise, we recall, had refused to marry Abelard partly because she refused to transform her freely given love into an obligation. So our author, whose doctoral bonnet is so much in evidence, rejoins one of the Middle Ages' greatest, and true, love stories.

The overwhelming passion of which Richard speaks may be extra- or nonmarital, but it is not courtly, at least in the narrow sense which modern scholars have sought to define. The *Advice* does not consider adultery a necessary ingredient; addressed to a young damsel, it has no thought of the remote *domna* of the Provençal lyric, the haughty lady whose cold, endless refusals bring endless suffering to the groveling suitor. Rather, the love it so enthusiastically advocates may be called romantic in the sense that it assumes the coloring and the principal motifs of the great twelfth-century French romances of which it is, in fact, a codification. Love as an overmastering force; love as mental conflict and anguish (described in words attributed to John of Garland, but more likely imperfect reminiscences of Alain de Lille); love as a *surprise*, totally unexpected, unwilled, unpremeditated; love in return toward the noble heart that loves one's own (whichever, man or woman, be stricken first), as a duty and as a necessity: all these aspects of love control the destinies of the heroes and heroines of the romances. Against his will and against his interests, Achilles is stricken with love for a woman, Polyxena, who cannot return his love. The result must be fatal (*Romance of Troy*). Lavinia, from her tower, espies her father's enemy, Aeneas, and is straightway wounded by Love's arrow (*Romance of Enéas*). Narcissus must die because he will not love Dané, who has been unexpectedly stricken with love for him (*Tale of Narcissus*). The examples of this curious law of reciprocation and of the other "laws" of love could be multiplied. Perhaps Tristan and Isolde should serve as supreme examples of the suffering of two beings surprised by love.

By Richard de Fournival's time, the great age of the romances was over; nor does he exist on their heroic plane. Where they depict their heroes as suffering all the torments of love that the poets had learned from Ovid, Richard now carefully observes that there are three stages in such agonies. With all his warmth and enthusiasm, he is a codifier of courtly love in the broader sense of the term, the passion of one noble being for another as distinguished from the mindless lusts of the herd. To the schematic tree of love which the schools had outlined, he gave the root of this love, "lady and queen of all the virtues." It is a tree that offers a curious parallel to the Trees of the Virtues, the Good Trees whose roots spring from Christian love; out of its stem "the flowers and fruits," in Richard's words, of the other virtues spring. But Richard probably saw no incongruity, nor did later poets, in adapting the religious imagery to profane purposes.

*Text:* The translation, which is complete save for the omission of a few trifling repetitions, is based on William M. McLeod, "The *Consaus d'Amours* of

Richard de Fournival," *Studies in Philology* 32
(1935): 1–21.[24]

BIBLIOGRAPHICAL NOTE

McLeod gives a brief life of Richard de Fournival in
his introduction. There appears to be no study of
the *Consaus:* McLeod does not discuss it. Paul
Klopsch, *Pseudo-Ovidius De Vetula, Untersu-
chungen und Text* (Leiden and Cologne, 1967), pp.
86 ff., gives a fuller biography.

Fair, gentle sister,

When I received your letter, in which you told me of your strong desire to be in love, I was indeed most pleased to learn of it; for you have now become a young lady, and one can see by your outward appearance that you are ready to sustain the demands of loving. I am, however, rather surprised by your request that I advise you on the means of undertaking love, and with whom. For, on such matters, none but your own heart can give counsel. And yet, because you are my sister and have confidence in me, and because it behooves me, as a good brother, to advise and instruct you, I shall comply with that part of your request which I find possible, and shall impart to you, by the written word, several facts which will help you begin to learn how to comport yourself while in love. My advice will, I believe, add much to what you learn from your own heart. Indeed, I am not so wise in this matter that I can teach you all there is to know about love; nor can any man alive do so. But I have heard a proverb which says: "Often a patient, almost a doctor"; and it is Virgil who tells us: "Happy the man made wise by others' misfortunes." [25] For this reason I shall write to you concerning those things which I myself have experienced from time to time, in the hope that you may learn much from them.

Now, therefore, I shall begin to discuss the subject, albeit rather briefly; for the memory is quick to falter, and it is sorely encumbered when one loads too much upon it. As Horace says:

"When you give precepts, take care to make them brief." [26] Man's heart retains a few words more readily than many. However, before entering upon the subject which is the reason for my writing, I should first like to speak to you about love in general. Afterwards, I shall move on to discuss, in orderly fashion, that special kind of love which is the subject of this work. For things which are set forth in proper order are the most easily understood.

In general, then, love is nothing more than a fervor of the mind, which directs the desires of the heart. As such, it can make itself felt for both good and ill; for under its power one may desire to perform either the one or the other. Thus it can be said that there are two kinds of love, good and evil. Evil love, however, is not really love at all. Indeed, it is nothing, just as a dead man is, in truth, not really a man. Good love, on the other hand, is real love. One calls it "virtue"; and it is of this that we speak when we describe love in the following manner.

Love is the virtue of virtues, a priceless quality, a shield against every vice and a bulwark against every danger. It is called "the virtue of virtues" not because it is lower than all others, or is subservient to them, but rather because it is above all other virtues, which are its subjects. For the other virtues are acquired in order that one may have love. Indeed, it is a well-known truth that one seeks those virtues for honor and self-interest. But, as Cicero tells us, self-interest must come second to love, not vice versa.[27] And so, since the other virtues follow self-interest, and since self-interest follows love, it is clear that all those virtues must follow love. That is why I dare say

RICHARD DE FOURNIVAL

that love is a highborn lady, queen of all the other virtues.

Love is said to be "a priceless quality" because it is so high and noble a virtue, of such great worth that none can judge it or accurately describe its powers. Cicero tells us: "Those who would banish love and friendship from the world would deprive it of the sun and its brilliance." [28] For God has given us no finer or more fortunate boon. Thus we may be sure that love is a truly exalted quality. Indeed, Ovid says that even nobility, highly esteemed though it be, is inferior to it.[29] Next I have said that love is "a shield against every vice." This is so because whoever has the virtue of love firmly implanted within him, can never give himself up to any wickedness or any act which might be turned to evil. In truth, the heart that is brightened by love shines with every good virtue; and virtue and vice are so opposed to one another that wherever virtue is found, no vice can intrude. I have told you also that love is "a bulwark against every danger"; for in performing a labor of love, one fears no peril whatever. For this reason Cicero says that love makes all things appear more clear and bright, and even makes the burdens of adversity easier to bear.[30]

This love which I have been discussing can be divided into two kinds: the spiritual and the temporal. As for the first, it seems to me that Cicero is speaking about such spiritual love when he says that love is a common feeling of compassion and good will for all things divine and human.[31] He speaks of "compassion and good will" because we ought never bear any ill will toward God or our fellow man. He speaks of "things divine and human" because we cannot truly love our Lord so long as we have hatred in our hearts for any man; nor can any other love be of value to us without the love of God. It is of this spiritual love that Saint John the Evangelist, and many another saint, speak in their books. But I shall not discuss it further at present, for I wish rather to enter upon the subject for which I have begun this letter. Nonetheless, fair sister, I pray that your heart ever hold this spiritual love within it, whatever else it may possess. For it will keep your heart at peace; and when the heart is at peace, one can rejoice and make merry all the better, and perform one's obligations all the more agreeably.

Now I shall speak about temporal love. Love is a kind of virtue by whose power we become well disposed to one and all. For we should never act toward another as we would not have him act toward us.[32] And this is a good virtue, and an easy one to maintain; for with it one achieves tranquillity, as well as worldly praise and success. This temporal love is of two kinds.

There is the kind of temporal love that comes directly from nature, and the kind that is born simply from the desire of the heart. The first is the love that exists between intimates, such as that which one feels for father, mother, family and lawful mate. The second is the love and kindly feeling that one feels toward the community of mankind. This latter love, in turn, is of two types: that which comes from a simple affection, and that which stems from a particular and deep-rooted desire. For the love born of simple affection is the common good will that one has for man in general; whereas, that born of a deep desire is the love that one bears for one person only, above all others. Nor can this love be felt for more than one; for the whole heart must give itself over to it, and the heart cannot be in many places at once. It is of this latter love especially that I wish to speak to you, since it is the reason for which I have undertaken the present discussion. Indeed, although it is the ultimate stage of love, nevertheless one must admit that all other kinds of love are born from this one. For it is the stem out of which the flowers and fruits of other loves spring, and it is the very root of all virtues and the substance of all good. It is, in truth, a very difficult thing to protect and preserve, for the conditions and circumstances propitious to this love of which I speak are themselves very difficult to maintain. For this reason one finds more who fail to preserve love than who succeed in sustaining it. Some fail to sustain it through lack of knowledge; but they are not to be so harshly blamed as others who do it ill through the wretched wickedness of their hearts, and who should be the object of our scorn. For God himself cursed with His own mouth all those who sow dissension and discord among men.[33] Indeed, it cannot be denied that wherever there is hate and enmity, there can be no love.

The essential quality of this love which is the root of all others, is that it must exist between male and female. It is obvious that this is as it should be. For the first love that God created upon this earth was, to be sure, between man and woman; and every day one can see that the love of man for woman, and of woman for man, moves the heart of each more than any other.

Dear sister, since the love of which I would speak to you is the root of every virtue and of every good act, it is fitting and proper that you give careful attention to what I tell you. Indeed, as a general rule, it is good to listen to everything and to learn all one can. Solomon tells us: "The more man hears, the wiser is he." [34] And the Holy Scriptures give this precept: "Experience all things, and what you find good, that shall you keep." [35] As I myself have learned from the reflections of Master John of Garland, this kind of love can be defined and described in the following manner.[36]

Love is a folly of the mind, an unquenchable fire, a hunger without surfeit, an agreeable illness, a sweet delight, a pleasing madness, a labor without repose and a repose without labor. You can see from this most wondrous and varied description of love that one must possess great skill to sustain it. No one finds it possible to offer a proper reason for such love, nor can anyone explain from whence it comes or how it is conceived in the heart, other than to say that it is a virtue born of the heart's unrestrained caprice. For this reason one finds that a king or gentleman of high degree may suddenly be moved to love a woman of low estate, and that a queen or highborn lady may well find herself, without warning, in love with a man of little worth. Just so, a poor man may dare to love a queen, and even a simple lass may dare to love a king. Indeed, love's capriciousness is such that reason does not even try to examine it. Therefore it is called "a folly of the mind"; for it gives itself freely, as does the sun, which would as soon shine upon the dungheap as upon the rosebush. Thus Ovid says that love observes no rules of good behavior, but does as it chooses; and if anyone attempts to hold it in check for any reason, then it persists all the more in doing what it will.[37] It is much like a fire, which will burn all the brighter the more it is stirred up. For this reason, the master calls it "an unquenchable fire." It is especially true that the more love is withheld, the more it is coveted; and the more one thinks about it, the more one wishes to do so. Therefore, the master calls it "a hunger without surfeit." And since those who love are often heartsick and wretched—for there is no yearning without woe—nevertheless, such woes are sweet and a delight to the heart. Thus love is called "an agreeable illness." And since the sweetness of love gladdens the heart and soothes the flesh, one says it is "a sweet delight." It appears, however, in so many diverse forms, that it resembles folly; and, indeed, this is why one calls it "a pleasing madness." Moreover, because it is a toilsome and arduous task to put aside all other thoughts for this one alone, love is said to be "a labor without repose." What is more, when one has suffered such ills and is able, at length, to cease his yearnings—having achieved his pleasure or the hopeful promise thereof—then is the heart so happy and content that it seems never to have suffered the slightest pain or woe and never to have labored at all in the winning of it; much like the woman, who forgets her every pain once she is delivered of her child. And it is for this reason, lastly, that love is called "a repose without labor."

When one has served love so well that he fulfills his heart's desire, it is, to be sure, a pleasing thing to gain the sweet repose of love. And although I could never in my life have the good fortune to earn love's gentle ease, yet, even when I have been so tormented by love that I could neither eat nor drink, sleep nor rest, even then I have never doubted the value of love and its sweet charms. So much was I comforted by hope in my yearning that I felt I was paying no price whatever. On the contrary, I found it so pleasing that it seemed to me that there was no other paradise than being in love; just like those souls in purgatory who fear neither their pain nor their anguish, so great is their hope for everlasting happiness. And since I found so much comfort in loving, despite the pain which it caused me, how much delight, joy, solace, peace and pleasure would I have found had I been fortunate enough to achieve the fulfillment of my desire! Indeed, there is no greater good than that which comes from loving loyally and well, nor any greater torment than from loving falsely.

Fair sister, I have explained the nature of love to the best of my knowledge. Now I should like to tell you in what manner love is conceived in the hearts of lovers, and how the heart must be disposed if it would conceive it. I pray that you give close attention to what I am about to tell you, and that you remember it well. I hope, also, that you will put it to good use; for knowledge is not given—or, should I say, entrusted—merely to be stored up, but rather so that it may serve a purpose. Remember what our Lord has said through the mouth of His prophet, of those men who learn wisdom and then do not make good use of it: "I have given them my gold and my silver, but with my gold and silver they fashion the devil and anger our Lord, and do what should not be done." [38] But perhaps you will object and say that there are many who condemn the practice of loving, and that in undertaking it you may risk much unpleasantness.

Let me assure you, however, that despite all those who choose to censure love, I for one shall always commend it to you, so long as you practice it according to the principles which I am about to set forth. I feel certain that those who listen to what I have to say will feel neither obliged nor able to reproach young persons who love each other, even if their actions should be unfit for public view. For tenderness of years is a sufficient excuse; and even our Lord, according to the Scriptures, pays less heed to the transgressions of youth than to all others.[39] It is well known that man's nature delights in dalliance and joyous merriment, pleasing to the flesh; and that in youth, nature should not be held in check. When one is too quick to deny his desires—especially those which spring from nature—he destroys the health of his body; and whoever mistreats his body to excess, commits an act against his very life. Moreover, I know of no reason to condemn love, so long as the love of our Lord be not forsworn, nor any ill be done to another. Whatever others may say, I hold that youthful dalliance is a pleasing thing; and I urge you, as does Ovid, to play while you yet have time. For the days and the years flow like the waters, ever downstream, never turning back; and there is no greater loss than the losing of time.[40] Other things may be recovered, but time, once lost, is gone forever. . . .

Therefore, fair maiden, as long as Time and Nature beckon, I urge you to go about their work. For I assure you that if you give yourself over to love, you will not be the worse for it, but indeed by far the better.

Next I would have you learn that love is conceived in a most wonderful manner; for it is, quite simply, a tender passion that wells up suddenly from the very depths of the heart. Such is its most proper origin. There are, however, three other sources of love: to wit, good repute, envy and greed. As for the first of these, it often comes to pass that a lady or a maiden will hear a man acclaimed and praised; and even if he is one for whom she would otherwise feel no affection, she will soon begin to long for him in her heart. Love conceived in this manner is not truly improper, although it is not so natural as the former. For, as I have said before, true love is so artless and unrestrained that it takes no pains to follow the dictates of reason, but chooses rather to act in any way it will.

The second of the three sources is envy. Thus there are some so ill behaved that, as soon as they see that one man loves a lady or a maiden, they too wish to love her; not through any heartfelt and tender affection, but only through an envious desire to wrong the other in any way they can. Love so conceived is evil beyond measure, and I would condemn to misery and torment all those who commit such wickedness, and any like them. The last of the three sources is the greedy hope of personal gain; for there are those who give themselves over to love in search of profit— money, jewels, land or anything else of value. In such love, however, there is no good at all. It is as Cicero says: "If one seeks love for its useful- ness, he will see love vanish as soon as its useful- ness ceases." The same author tells us that true love is love with no desire for gain whatever; for when one seeks profit through loving, it is not love at all, but merely commerce.[41]

Now that I have recounted for you the ways in which love may be conceived, I should like to tell you the qualities that hearts must possess if love is to dwell within them. To begin, a lover's heart must abound in nobility of thought and deed. This nobility is a kind of grace that one finds, perforce, in those possessed of certain excellent qualities, the first of which is humility. As our Lord has said in the Gospel: "He that humbles himself shall be exalted." [42] To be humble is to be gracious and pleasing. Contrariwise, there is no quality in man so hateful as haughtiness; nor is there anyone so fair, rich or generous that he is not hated and despised if he is overproud. For haughty pride and humility are enemies of one another. To be sure, it was through their pride that the angels were cast down from Heaven and into the abyss. In short, if one would love, let him not be haughty. It is Ovid who tells us: "Pride and love cannot dwell together." [43] Another excellent quality that lovers must possess is refinement, a virtue which imparts much grace and elegance. This refinement of which I speak is the source of tender passion, and it is free of envy, the root of all evil. In the words of Aristotle: "Envy is a vice so foul and ugly that it is not to be found in any righteous heart." [44] Likewise Ovid declares that, although one may find some enjoyment in other vices, in this vice there is no enjoyment whatever. Nor can the heart know greater torment than when it is envious; for, indeed, when one feels envy, he torments none but himself. A similar observation is made by Horace.[45] Still another excellent quality that a lover must possess is gentility. It is this attribute that preserves one from all conduct worthy of censure. For gentility protects man from falling into baseness, helps him to maintain a fair appearance and behavior, and keeps him from indulging in an annoying excess of meaningless prattle. Tactfulness is yet another necessary quality. It is, quite simply, a certain awareness of how one should behave; and it is one of the most important qualities and pleasing traits that anyone may possess. Through tactfulness one learns how to keep secret things which should not be revealed. Indeed, one always risks the loss of sound judgment by talking too much.

For excessive talk, the philosopher tells us,[46] is a vice that mankind finds most vexing, since anyone who cannot long be still is quite unable to keep a secret: the tongue, in truth, is a slippery and unruly little organ. And so, fair sister, let me warn you never to give your trust to a man who talks more than he ought. The final quality that a lover should possess, if he would achieve the nobility of which I speak, is sincere and steadfast honesty, the foundation of all proper conduct. It is the luster of love and its most constant adornment. Without this quality all others are worthless, for it is this one that strengthens and sustains the rest. Now you have learned all the excellent qualities with which nobility of thought and deed is invested, and you know that the heart in which such nobility shines forth is a worthy dwelling place for love. As Virgil says, love shuns the lowly hearts and seeks out the lofty.[47]

I have already described for you the manner in which love is conceived. Let me make clear, as well, that either man or woman may be the first to love; sometimes the one, sometimes the other. And yet, love always follows the same path, whether it be man's love for woman or woman's for man.

You know too, of course, that the heart is the abode of love, because every good virtue dwells within it. Now I must tell you, however, that although man wins the love of lady or maiden by his earnest entreaty or through the esteem in

EYES

which he is held, nevertheless it is the eyes which are the true pathway to love. For the eyes are the windows of the heart; and through them, one can see deep within it. Unlike the mouth, the eyes can tell no lie. And so, when it happens that a man casts amorous glances toward the object of his desire, the lady—if her heart is worthy of loving—will perceive the love that calls out to her; and, yielding to his nobility, a quality of which I have spoken at length, she will welcome his love into her heart. For no proper heart can refuse to let love dwell within it.

In such a manner, then, does love go forth from the eyes of one to enter the eyes of another, in whose heart it then implants itself. There are many who marvel that this should be so. But indeed, they need find little cause for wonder: love, being the queen of all virtues, has powers which all the others lack. Moreover, let them consider this: Aristotle, in his discussion of the nature of animals, tells us about the basilisk, a beast whose venom is so strong and powerful that, with a simple glance, he can poison and kill all who gaze upon him.[48] If, therefore, we find among the evil forces of nature one more powerful than all the rest, we should not marvel to find among the virtuous powers one that surpasses all others. And, to be sure, love does have much power that the other virtues do not possess, besides what you have already heard. It is of such strength that it can do what no other virtue in the world can do; for its strength is such, as Virgil says, that it conquers all things.[49]

At this point I wish to teach you about the three stages of love: nascent, declared and consummated. Nascent love is that tenderness first conceived in the hearts of man or woman, the beginning of a mutual sympathy and desire. Declared love is affection openly offered and accepted by both—that singleness of will that one feels when the man becomes the lady's special friend, and she his. Consummated love is reached when the desires of both achieve complete fulfillment in kiss and embrace. There are those, too, who would say that there exists a fourth stage of love, namely permanent love, which leads to a marriage sanctified by the sacraments of the holy church. But whatever they say, I insist that such is not properly a stage of the love here under discussion. For married love is like a debt which one must pay, while the love of which I speak is a kind of grace freely bestowed. Although it is a mark of good manners to pay what one owes, still, there is no more delightful love than that born of the gratuitous favor of an artless, ingenuous heart.

Since you now know the three stages of love, you must learn also that in love there are three kinds of sickness. The first is known as the "love-sick fever." The second is the "restless affliction"; and the third, the "transforming disease." "Love-sick fever" is an illness that befalls those newly afflicted with a yearning heart. That is, when one takes it into his mind to love, and must debate with himself whether he shall do so or not; and if so, how he shall go about it. Such reflections chase all other thoughts and desires from his mind. They rob him of all appetite, sleep and repose, until, at length, he begins to grow pale, just as if he were suffering from a veritable fever.[50] The "restless affliction" is a sickness that lovers must endure when they cannot long remain in one place, but wish, rather, to go again and again where their heart longs to be. And there are some who jokingly call this sickness "Saint James's disease." [51] The "transforming disease" is the illness that lovers suffer when they seem to have lost their memory and mind; for they lose all sense of proper behavior and bearing, and shun the company of one and all, wishing no other solace than the thought of their love. These, then, are the three kinds of lovesickness. Perhaps some will ask, if love is as excellent a quality as I have stated, and the seat of so many noble virtues, how it can be that one finds within it such pain and heartache.

To this question I reply that, whereas other illnesses afflict man through a perturbation of certain bodily humors that sustain life, the illnesses of love come from no such impairment or disorder—for lovesickness is unlike any other—but rather from the great yearnings that weigh heavily upon the heart. And just as one has, on occasion, seen those whose joy is so intense that they can neither eat nor drink, and so die from their emotion, so too does the longing of love cause the illnesses which I have described to you.

Now that you have learned what I have had to say thus far, I should like to explain to you the reasons for which love, once conceived, may be slow of fruition, and the remedies that one may use to bring such delay to an end. Either man or woman may be to blame for allowing love to remain unfulfilled. The fault lies with the man in the following circumstances: Let us say that he has begun to love a lady, but that she is unaware of his affection, either because she is so secluded or closely guarded that she has no opportunity to speak with him, or because she is such a highborn lady that he dare not confess his desires. If the former, he must then seek some artful stratagem by which to put his amorous request before her, either in the words of a messenger or in writing. On the other hand, should the latter reason obtain, he must find means to gain the highborn lady's interest and favor, so much that she will, in time, deign to hear him speak. Once he has found that she is willing to give him ear, then he must fill his speech with tales of love, and the joys and solace that love can bring. At length, in the midst of his discourse, he will find the proper moment to speak in his own behalf; and, summoning up all his courage, he will proclaim his distress in passionate entreaty: "Milady, you are the light and the joy of my heart, the hope of my life. You may do with me what you will, for yours is the power of life and death over me. I am your servant, ready to do your bidding. Milady, I pray to God that you take no offense if I confess to you, as I must, that I love you with all my heart. And so I beseech you, Milady, for God's sake, to keep me as your faithful friend and servant; else all the good that is in you and all the noble love that dwells within my heart will have brought me to my death."

So it is that the suitor must entreat the lady in as pleasing, and yet as bold, a manner as possible. As the poet says: "Fortune favors the bold." [52] Thus the man should be serious and straightforward in voicing his distress; for, when one is miserable, one has the right to seek a remedy. Moreover, you may be sure that, however displeased the lady may appear, she will be far less vexed with the suitor than she seems—highborn though she be—even if she may not choose to love him in return. Indeed, it is most unfitting to repay good with evil or love with hate. Furthermore, whoever and whatever the man may be, the lady loses nothing if he loves her, since she is free to spurn his love if she thinks it best to do so.

Sometimes, as I have said, when love is not fulfilled, the fault lies with the lady; for she may love a gentleman, and yet he may not know it. Here is what she must do if such be the case. She must call his attention to herself in any number of ways: by speaking to him of some vague concern; by feigning love in obvious jest; by long, affectionate glances; or by pleasant, courteous speech. In short, by anything but a frank and open entreaty. For I shall never deem it proper that woman be the pursuer and man the pursued. And yet, she may affect all other artful guises to disclose her love. If the man is so dim-witted that he fails to perceive it, so much the worse for him.

There is another manner in which woman may delay the joy of love's fulfillment; namely, when she tarries too long in granting a suitor's amorous requests. This is a most unseemly thing to do, unless there is a good reason for it. Yet many are the ladies who, although they yearn to give their love, still hold it back hoping to be wooed all the more, as if it were a kind of game with them. Let me tell you that it is an odious, ill-mannered and, indeed, a sinful thing for ladies to make a suitor languish on and on in this way, as if they would traffic in love and sell it for a price. For there is nothing more dearly bought than the things one acquires by lengthy supplication; nor is there any greater pain in this world than endless waiting. Moreover, there can be—and, in truth, there have often been—many dangers in such procrastination. A lady may drive her lover to despair thereby, and lose him altogether. Then too, the more he must prolong his entreaty, the greater is the risk that the entire affair may be disclosed.

*Advice on Love*

For man is never so wary while in the heat of pursuit as he is once he has reached his goal. Indeed, when one is laying siege to a castle, he thinks of nothing save the attack. It is only after it has been taken that he takes pains to keep it secure. Thus we read in Lucan that we should put aside delay, for nothing vexes more than needless waiting.[53] Ovid, in turn, tells us that delay can be the source of much distress, and that those who tarry unduly in giving what should be given, are worthy of great blame.[54] And so, in his wisdom, the Sage counsels us never to tell the friend who seeks a boon which we can easily accord straightway: "Return tomorrow, you shall have it then." [55] Thus, as I have said, it is wrong to delay what can be done at once, unless for a good cause.

Now let me reveal to you the proper reason for which a lady may, in fact, withhold the gift of her love. Let us say that a lady is wooed by a man, and yet knows him not at all. In this case she must not be too quick to give her love, for undue haste is most unseemly. Rather should she keep him in uncertainty, neither granting his request nor refusing it, until she may be certain of his character and his behavior, and until she may know that his protestations of love are true and his heart sincere. For there are some men who go wooing out of habit, and who can find no other way to act with a lady or a maiden than to begin at once to pay her court. Such men have as many true loves as they have lady friends. They are like the swallow, who takes neither food nor drink except while in flight. For these suitors do all their loving on the wing; nor will they ever bring their heart to rest in any single place, although they will always profess that their whole heart is in each new acquaintance that they make. Indeed, I should gladly see the hearts of such men ripped forcibly from their bodies, for no good can come from knowing them; nor do they shrink from any action, come what may, so long as they may do their will. One must be wary of such men as these. I pray, fair sister, that you will be so, and that you will keep in mind the words of Isidore: "Beware of those who seem disposed to good, even more than those who seem disposed to evil."[56] In truth, the Trojans were deceived and betrayed by a horse brought into their midst, which had the appearance of one of their divinities. It is easy to guard against those who seem inclined to evil, for they are clearly recognized. But those who seem inclined to good, while in truth they are evil, work their deceit without delay. They are like the fox, who, feigning death, lies motionless in the middle of the road with his tongue hanging out. When the magpies, thinking him dead, come to feast on his tongue, he bares his teeth, catches one and quickly does it in.[57] Many men know how to practice such trickery; for they will beseech a maiden or a lady for her love so humbly and piteously, and they will feign distress so well, that they will seem to be on the very point of death. They will be so smooth of speech—like all who are well versed in this art—that they will win the love they seek more quickly than the true and loyal suitor, whose heart is so heavy with love that only with great difficulty will he dare bring himself to disclose the need that torments him. For you will never find a true and loyal lover, clever though he be, and certain of the way in which he will make known his desire, who does not fall speechless with awe when he comes before his lady. It is for this reason that I warn you never to trust in the love of a man who bares his heart to you boldly, with no restraint and no discomfiture. On the other hand, it is also very possible to recognize a true and loyal lover; for when he is before you he will be artless, pensive and full of sighing. He will have a piteous and loving glance; and when he gazes at you, it will seem that he is about to laugh and cry all at once. Indeed, this is one of the surest and most pleasing ways to prove the sincerity of a suitor's heart.

This, then, is the reason why a lady, at times, should withhold her love; to wit, until she comes to know the disposition and behavior of the one who seeks it. Once she is certain of his proper character, she should receive him graciously and with good cheer. It follows that, if your love is sought by one whom you know without question to be of good character and bearing, you may accord it at once; that is, so long as you have not already granted it to another. For it would not truly be love if it were given freely here, there and everywhere. There is a proverb that says: "Only he who knows an herb should use it to cure his eye." [58] Nor should you be like some women who seem to imitate the ways of the wolf. This animal is of such nature that he prefers to find his prey far from his lair rather than close to it. In like manner, some women would sooner love a stranger than a man whom they already know.[59] Those who are close to them they hold in scorn, much like the woman who, it is said, would not kneel down before the crucifix made from the tree that grew in her own garden. Women who seek such distant loves do not really know what love is, nor what joy it can bring. As the maxim tells us: "It is wise to love your neighbor's daughter, for you see her by night and by day." Indeed, it is well for a woman to love a man whom she sees often, for she may thereby observe his behavior each day, and see whether he conducts himself in a proper or unseemly manner. Remember too that, once you have a faithful and loving friend, you should not be quick to believe whatever evil may be said about him. Nowhere do slanderers ply their mischief more willingly than between lovers, and many a person has often been maligned although he has been guilty of no fault whatever. You must keep in mind, also, that if your friend should suffer the misfortune of sickness or poverty, or if his duties force him to go far away and leave you for a long time, still you must not give up your love or allow yourself to forget him. It is for this reason that Master Pierre de Blois has said: "Love is something that cannot be altered by absence, put asunder by distance, destroyed by misfortune, nor can it be harmed in any way." [60]

Fair, gentle sister, I prefer not to write any more in this fashion; for, in truth, I have never learned so much that I ought dare discuss the rest of this subject with you. It is so difficult to pursue the matter of love further, that I fear lest I should err in it. And yet, if you remember well what I have told you, your heart itself will teach you all the rest there is to know. The proverb tells us: "Bird of good breeding teaches itself"; and I feel that you are of such nature that you will, by your own heart alone, be able to prepare yourself for what comes after. Only keep in mind the lessons that I have given you here, brief though they be; for I have wished to make them short enough so that your memory might more easily retain them.

It is better to know a few of wisdom's commandments and be able to make use of them when necessary, than to learn so many that one cannot remember any of them. To be sure, he who would learn to be a proper man-at-arms must not try to master every thrust and parry. Let him learn but two or three good blows to use against an adversary: he will be the better served by them in time of need. Thus I believe that you will, if necessary, remember the few lessons which I have written here, more easily than a greater number with which I might have burdened you. And so, at the conclusion of my work, I urge and counsel you, good sister, for the affection in which I hold you, never to be without love. Always try, rather, to love faithfully, with a heart free of all deceit. If you do this well and steadfastly, you will not fail to have joy, honor and advantage thereby. This you will learn from the adventure which I shall now relate.[61]

When I myself was yet a raw and callow knight, I was as scornful of love as any man could be. Never had I seen a maiden or lady, however beautiful or worthy, in whom I wished to place the affection of my heart. For I held love in such low esteem that it seemed to me a thing of no value. In truth, when I would hear men lament that they were dying of love, I believed that it was an invention and a mere pleasantry. At length, God wished to instruct me, and he made me conceive the desire of going off in search of adventure, as was the custom of every knight-errant. And so I set out, for I was but new to knighthood; and being yet unproven in every way, I wished to prove myself in some worthy adventure. So it was that I came to find myself in the Forest of Long Reflection, where I did, indeed, encounter fine and wondrous adventures aplenty. One of these led me to the court of the god of love.

It would take far too long to tell you here the manner in which I was received, and all the marvels I witnessed there. Suffice it to relate that, because I had never been in love, I was not allowed to enter the great inner hall. I was, however, permitted the favor of remaining outside and looking at the wonders within. And because it was, that day, the feast of the Ascension, the god of love was holding court in high and noble fashion.

The hall was so beautiful and of such pleasing elegance that I do not believe the earthly paradise could have been compared with it. The god of love was within, and with him a retinue of loyal lovers, each with his lady friend. No mouth can relate, nor any pen describe, the games, frolics and delights that they performed therein. In truth, it gave me such pleasure merely to witness them, that I would gladly have remained there for the rest of my days. At length, I asked an old man who was standing guard at the entrance to the great hall what people these were, who were reveling in such a manner; and he answered that the god of love was honoring his loyal lovers with joyous sport and merriment.

While speaking to this worthy old man, I looked up and saw a goodly number of men and women passing into the inner courtyard. All of them were almost naked, being clothed only in their shirts. Thereupon the followers of the god of love led them toward a pool which was in the middle of the courtyard and whose water was all turned to ice. Upon the ice there were many stools, all fashioned out of sharp and prickly thorns, and the men and women were made to sit upon them. The thorns were very sharp indeed, and wounded them so deeply that their crimson blood gushed forth in abundance. At the same time, their feet became frozen into the ice and caused them such great distress that they moaned and shrieked in a manner most piteous to hear. All the while the others stood by them, crying out: "Now at last your evil ways will have their just deserts."

I was most amazed to see these things, and I asked the old man who was guarding the entrance to the hall what, indeed, was happening, and what people these were. He replied that they were the men and women who had done great violence to love by yielding their hearts and bodies to many and sundry. For this reason the god of love was repaying them their due recompense, as I have described it, and one which they would continue to receive all the days of their lives.

While he was explaining these things to me, a bolt of lightning rent the air, so bright that it seemed that all the earth was consumed in smoke and flame; and I heard such a loud noise that I believed the heavens above would come falling to the ground. At that moment, hearing a great commotion, I turned my eyes to see what it might be, and saw many men and women riding over the bridge which led to the entrance of the court. Their heads were bare, and they were clad in black tunics so short that they did not touch the knee, and whose sleeves did not even reach to the elbow. Their feet were unshod, and the fleshless nags on which they were riding, with no saddle of any kind upon their bare backs, were galloping so heavily that the chattering of their teeth sounded like the pounding of many hammers. The air was full of rain and hailstones that came showering down upon the riders and their mounts with such force, that it was, indeed, a fearful sight to behold. As soon as they had passed through the gate, the servants greeted them with sharp-pointed goads with which they jabbed and pricked them; and they continued to do so until all the men and women had been forced into a horrible pit within the inner court-yard. And this pit was so dark and foul-smelling that it seemed a very inferno; for all the filth—from the kitchen and other parts of the court as well—was cast down into it.

Then the servants began to shout: "Now are all you evil folk repaid for your sinful arro-gance." And as I heard these amazing things I was so awe-struck that I trembled with fright and almost lost the use of all my limbs. I inquired of the worthy old man what people these were; whereupon he replied that they were the men and women who had been—and, indeed, still were—so full of haughty pride that they never wished to be in love. Their recompense was such as I have described it, and so it would be for the rest of their lives. Then he said to me: "Dear friend, if you take my advice you will leave this place at once, lest any who see you here do you grievous injury. For I know that you are not worthy to remain here; and indeed, God has done you great kindness even to let you stay and see all these things. Now be off! And in the future, try to lead a better life than you have done here-tofore, and one which will earn the favor of my lord the god of love. For you may be sure that, at present, he holds you in mortal hatred."

When I heard these words I took my leave as

fast as I was able. Returning to my horse, which I had left tied to a tree, I mounted him and began my homeward journey. And you may be sure that I, who had always been so haughty and proud toward love, did not rest until my heart had learned to love loyally and well. I pray, fair sister, that you may do likewise.

For none can describe to you the great joys and pleasures that true lovers know, who dwell with the god of love; nor the torment and pain of those who love falsely, and those who do not wish to love at all. I pray that God may show you the path to true and loyal loving, and that you may enjoy and profit from it. I pray, too, that you beseech God in my favor, that in days to come He may, in His mercy, let me take pleasure in the delights of love.

# Notes

1. C. S. Lewis, *The Allegory of Love* (New York, 1958), p. 4.

2. Gaston Paris launched the expression in his "Études sur les romans de la Table Ronde. *Lancelot du Lac*. II. *Le Conte de la Charrette*," in *Romania* 12 (1883):459–534.

3. Peter Dronke, *Mediæval Latin and the Rise of the European Love Lyric*, 2 vols. (Oxford, 1965–66), 1:9 ff., 39. Also, D. W. Robertson, Jr., "The Concept of Courtly Love as an Impediment to the Understanding of Medieval Texts," in F. X. Newman, ed., *The Meaning of Courtly Love* (Albany, N.Y., 1968).

4. Guillelmi Abbatis Sancti Theoderici, *Tractatus de natura et de dignitate amoris*, in J. P. Migne, ed., *Patrologia Latina*, CLXXXIV, col. 381 (hereafter cited as Migne, *PL*).

5. See E. K. Rand, *Ovid and His Influence* (Boston, 1925), p. 112. Also, L. P. Wilkinson, *Ovid Surveyed* (Cambridge, 1962), p. 182.

6. Still of interest in this regard is the study of Gaston Paris, "Chrétien Legouais et autres traducteurs ou imitateurs d'Ovide," in *Histoire littéraire de la France* 29 (1885):455–525.

7. An early and influential Christianizing of Cicero is St. Ambrose, *De officiis ministrorum*, cap. xxi, xxii, in Migne, *PL*, LXVI, cols. 179–84. For text of Aelred of Rievaulx, *De spirituali amicitia*, see Migne, *PL*, CVC. The texts of Pierre de Blois, *De amicitia christiana* and *De dilectione Dei et proximi*, are published in M. M. Davy, *Un Traité de l'amour du XIIe siècle: Pierre de Blois* (Paris, 1932).

Pierre de Blois, secretary to Henry II and Eleanor of Aquitaine, expressly condemns the literary fashion of romantic love cultivated at their courts (*De amicitia christiana*, cap. vi, "De carnali amore"). For editions of other authors mentioned here, the reader is referred to the appropriate chapters of the present collection.

8. The author of the *Key* could have had no direct knowledge of Homer. His reference is perhaps a garbled reminiscence of Virgil (the story of Dido) and Ovid *Ars amatoria* 2. 123–24 ("Ulysses was not handsome, but he was elegant . . .").

9. Aigremore was the residence of the Emir Balant, who, according to the Old French epics, destroyed Rome. One poem places it "in the islands of Majorca, where lives a foul race of men."

10. It was generally accepted that "stags . . . after a dinner of snake . . . shed their coats and all their old age with them" (T. H. White, trans. and ed., *The Bestiary, a Book of Beasts, Being a Translation of a Latin Bestiary of the Twelfth Century* [New York, 1960], p. 38).

11. Numerous apocryphal works were attributed to Aristotle. The reference here is perhaps to the *Secreta secretorum*, an immensely popular compilation. It is analyzed by Charles-Victor Langlois, in *La Connaissance de la nature et du monde* (Paris, 1927), pp. 71–121.

12. Matt. 6:24.

13. The poet refers to heroes of twelfth-century epics and romances. Roland, Oliver, and Gawain are well known. Horn is the hero of *Horn et Rimel;* Ipomedon, of a romance which bears his name.

14. That Robert de Blois intends this and similar practical advice to be taken seriously may be gathered from one of Europe's most famous courtesy books, the *Galateo* of Giovanni della Casa (1558). See the translation by R. S. Pine-Coffin (London, 1958), in which the "Note on Books of Courtesy in England" (pp. 105–31) shows how widespread

was the need for such advice, and for how many centuries.

15. In medieval times, before the Communion, the priest and the people would kiss the *pax* ("peace"), a tablet bearing a symbol or figure of Christ, the Virgin Mary, or a specific saint.

16. The proverb which concludes Robert's manuscript—"Car quant plus giele, plus estroint"— appears in the medieval collection *Li Proverbe au vilain,* ed. A. Tobler (Leipzig, 1895). In the present context it seems to suggest that the more passionately a lover loves his lady, the more faithful will he remain to her.

17. Andreas means his rule to apply to both sexes.

18. In the original, Andreas uses the verb "to love" actively, not passively, "to be loved," as in Drouart.

19. Andreas's rule, unlike Drouart's, applies to the survivor of either sex.

20. Drouart's version makes this rule very similar to the fifth. In addition, he restricts it to one sex, whereas Andreas intends it for both.

21. In Andreas's corresponding rule, speaking is not mentioned.

22. Andreas's symptoms are more specific: the lover's heart palpitates.

23. The final assurance that, despite his suspicions, the lover does not hate the beloved, is an addition of Drouart's.

24. Of all the texts in this volume, *Advice on Love* invites, and indeed requires, the most annotation. The margins of the manuscript contain Latin quotations that correspond to Richard de Fournival's French translation of lines from ancient poets and prose writers, and of verses from the Bible. These Latin quotations are not always accurate, nor are they all to be found in the authors to whom they are attributed. The modern editor of the *Advice,* William M. McLeod, did his best to seek out the original sources, but in so doing he made Richard de

Fournival appear more of a classical scholar than he was. Richard's quotations are of the kind learned by rote in the schools—quotations for all occasions, the commonplaces of wisdom, and so forth. Almost all are desperately trite, as a glance at collections of medieval proverbs and aphorisms will readily confirm. The tone of the *Advice* is more in harmony with its own age, more "medieval," than learned footnote references to the ancients might lead one to suspect.

25. The attribution to Virgil is incorrect. J. Morawski attributes the saying to Cato in his edition of the *Diz et proverbes des sages* (Paris, 1924), p. 19, st. 10. See also pp. 5–6. H. Walther's *Proverbia sententiæque latinitatis medii ævi: Lateinische Sprichtwörter und Sentenzen des Mittelalters in alphabetischer Anordnung* (Göttingen, 1963–67), lists numerous occurrences of the Latin version under no. 8952.

26. Horace *Ars poetica* 11. 335–36. Numerous entries in Walther, *Proverbia*, no. 25309.

27. Cicero *De amicitia* 14. 51.

28. Ibid., 13. 47 (inaccurately quoted).

29. Ovid *Epist.* 4. 161. Walther, *Proverbia*, no. 17033.

30. Cicero *De amicitia* 6. 22.

31. This is the often-repeated Ciceronian definition of friendship, "Est autem amicitia nihil aliud nisi omnium divinarum humanarumque rerum cum benevolentia et caritate consensio" (*De amicitia* 6. 20). The words themselves invite those so inclined to make a Christian interpretation.

32. The editor suggests Tobit 4. 16, but the saying was proverbial. The very widely known *Disticha Catonis*, translated by Elye de Wincestre, says "A autrui fai cum vuols a tei." See E. Stengel, ed., *L'Afaitement Catun* (Marburg, 1886), p. 114, l. 73.

33. Matt. 18:17.

34. Prov. 1:15.

35. 1 Thess. 5:21.

36. John of Garland (died ca. 1260), Paris master, grammarian, and poet, was author, *inter alia*, of commentaries on Ovid and a *Poetria* (a manual on the composition of poetry). The antithetical definition of love ascribed to him recalls a famous passage of the *Complaint of Nature* of Alain de Lille, *doctor universalis* (died 1202).

37. Ovid *Epist.* 4. 154. Walther, *Proverbia*, no. 24996.

38. Hos. 2:8 (but garbled).

39. Vulg. Ps. 24:7 (AV, Ps. 25:7: "Remember not the sins of my youth, nor my transgressions . . . for thy goodness' sake, O Lord"). Such is the marginal reference in the manuscript of the *Advice*. Richard makes a rather particular application.

40. Ovid *Ars amatoria* 3. 62–64. Walther, *Proverbia*, no. 14053. On loss of time, see Seneca *De brevitate vitæ* 8.

41. Cicero *De amicitia* 9. 32; 27. 100.

42. Matt. 23:12; Luke 14:11 and 18:14.

43. Ovid *Metamorphoses* 2. 846–47.

44. The reference to Aristotle has not been identified.

45. A paraphrase of Ovid *Metamorphoses* 2. 760 ff.; also Horace *Epist.* 1. 2. 58.

46. The "philosopher" is Aristotle; the idea, a commonplace.

47. The source, not in Virgil, remains unidentified.

48. See T. H. White, *The Bestiary*, pp. 68–69, for information on this piece of nature lore.

49. Virgil *Eclogue* 10. 69: "Omnia vincit amor," a tag so familiar that its source is often forgotten.

50. Greek physicians and their Arab successors regularly discussed love as a physical disease. See, for example, J. L. Lowes, "The Loveres Maladye of Hereos," in *Modern Philology* 11, no. 4 (1914): 1–56.

51. A sly reference to the immense popularity of

the pilgrimage to Saint James of Compostella and to the less than pious conduct for which the journey offered opportunities. "Qui bon y part, mauvais revient," it was commonly said.

52. Virgil *Aeneid* 10. 281: "Fortuna audaces iuvat." The idea was proverbial, however. Cf. "Fortune secourt les hardiz" (*Roman de Renart*), quoted by Antoine Le Roux de Lincy, *Le Livre des proverbes français*, 2 vols. (Paris, 1859), 2:301. See also Walther, *Proverbia*, no. 9844a.

53. Lucan *Pharsalia* 1. 280–81: "Tolle moras, semper nocuit differe paratis." The idea, however, is commonplace. See Morawski, *Diz et proverbes*, p. 10, st. 24, where it is attributed to Seneca and, by two manuscripts, to Solomon.

54. Unidentified reference to Ovid.

55. The "Sage" is Solomon, Prov. 3:28. (The King James version gives "neighbor" rather than "friend.") The advice was often quoted, and even attributed to Seneca. See Morawski, *Diz et proverbes*, p. 11, st. 32, and note, p. 114.

56. Saint Isidore of Seville, famous seventh-century encyclopedist. The exact reference has not been traced.

57. See T. H. White, *The Bestiary*, p. 54, for a discussion of this trick, characteristic of many played by Reynard the Fox. The allegorists saw in him a type of the devil.

58. Le Roux de Lincy, *Le Livre des proverbes*, 1: 76–77, quotes this proverb: "Qui l'erbe conoist doit on mettre en son oeul"; but he has difficulty in explaining it. The present context seems to call for a translation like the one given; namely, that only one who is skilled in the use of an herb should try to use it medicinally.

59. Brunetto Latini, in *Le Livre du trésor*, explains that wolves copulate only twelve days a year, when the female chooses the ugliest male of the pack, and, to protect her young, hunts only in distant territory. (See A. Pauphilet, *Jeux et sapience du*

*moyen âge* [Paris, 1951], p. 817.) Richard de Four-
nival seems to have confused the facts.

60. This definition is Ciceronian (*De amicitia* 7.
23), though garbled. It is found in Pierre de Blois
(died ca. 1200). See M. M. Davy, *Un Traité de
l'amour*, p. 117.

61. The episode that follows is clearly dependent
upon the Fifth Dialogue of Andreas Capellanus. See
*The Art of Courtly Love*, trans. and ed. John Jay
Parry (New York, 1941), pp. 68 ff.

Norman R. Shapiro is associate professor of Romance languages and literatures at Wesleyan University. He received his B.A., M.A., and Ph.D. from Harvard University and has taught there and at Amherst College. He is co-editor of *Échos* (1965), a college French reader, editor and translator of *Negritude: Black Poetry from Africa and the Caribbean* (1970), and translator of *Four Farces of Georges Feydeau* (1970).

James B. Wadsworth is professor and chairman of the department of Romance languages at Tufts University. He received his M.A. and Ph.D. from Harvard University and has taught there and at Queens College and Pennsylvania State University. His previous publications include *Lyons, 1470–1503: The Beginnings of Cosmopolitanism; Symphorien Champier: Le Livre de vraye amour;* and several articles on the French Middle Ages and Renaissance.

UNIVERSITY OF ILLINOIS PRESS

T